LIBYA AND QADDAFI

LIBYA AND QADDAFI

A REVISED EDITION
BY DON LAWSON

FRANKLIN WATTS
NEW YORK I LONDON I TORONTO I SYDNEY I 1987
AN IMPACT BOOK

Frontis: on this stretch of barren desert in Libya stands a lone oil-drilling rig. Oil was first discovered in this nation in 1958.

Map by Vantage Art, Inc.

Photographs courtesy of:
UPI/Bettmann Newsphotos: pp. 2, 19, 34, 40, 106;
Reuters/Bettmann Newsphotos: pp. 11 (top), 23, 29, 65, 118;
U.S. Air Force Photo: p. 8 (top);
AP/Wide World Photos: pp. 8 (bottom), 11 (bottom), 14, 17, 25, 26, 37, 45, 49, 55, 57, 62, 103;
The Bettmann Archive: pp. 35, 75, 80, 89, 93;
Culver Pictures: p. 78.

Library of Congress Cataloging-in-Publication Data

Lawson, Don.
Libya and Qaddafi.

(An Impact book)
Bibliography: p.
Includes index.
Summary: Discusses the recent history of Libya and the background of current issues in its relations with the United States and other countries, as well as the role played by the strongman Qaddafi.
1. Libya—Juvenile literature. 2. Qaddafi, Muammar— Juvenile literature. [1. Libya. 2. Qaddafi, Muammar] I. Title.
DT215.L38 1987   961'.204   86-28211
ISBN 0-531-10329-3

CONTENTS

LIBYA AND QADDAFI

Above: *an F-111 aircraft. Mounted on the aircraft's wing pylons are four laser-guided missiles. Below: an A-6E Intruder aircraft. The A-6E is able to carry over thirty types of weapons and operates day or night, regardless of weather conditions.*

ONE

THE UNITED STATES BOMBS LIBYA

During the dark predawn hours of April 14, 1986, U.S. Air Force and Navy warplanes suddenly launched a devastating bomb attack against the North African nation of Libya. Making the attack were thirteen U.S. Air Force F-111 fighter-bombers and a dozen Navy A-6 attack planes. The F-111's had flown all the way from their air bases in Great Britain, and the A-6's had been launched from U.S. aircraft carriers in the Mediterranean Sea.

Although the air raid lasted for less than fifteen minutes, it destroyed several key military targets and caused several hundred casualties in and near the Libyan cities of Tripoli and Benghazi. Among the places destroyed was a building where Libya's controversial dictator, Muammar Qaddafi, lived and had his command communications headquarters. Qaddafi himself was not among the casualties, but he and his wife, Safia, claimed that two of their three sons had been wounded and a fifteen-month-old adopted daughter, Hana, had been killed.

One U.S. F-111 and its two-man crew were reported lost in the attack. The missing crewmen were the pilot,

Captain Fernando L. Ribas-Dominicci, and the weapons officer, Captain Paul L. Lorence. A few days later it was reported that the body of one of the two missing airmen had washed ashore and that the Libyans were demanding a ransom or concessions from the United States before they would return it. Washington would neither confirm nor deny this report. Several weeks later it was reported that the body of the second missing crewman had washed ashore near Benghazi.

WHY LIBYA WAS BOMBED

The United States claimed that the purpose of the air raid was to prevent any more terrorist attacks from being launched by Libya against American citizens abroad. Just a week earlier La Belle discotheque, a nightclub in West Berlin frequented by U.S. servicemen and women, had been bombed. In this terrorist attack an American soldier, Sergeant Kenneth T. Ford, was killed and some fifty other American military personnel were wounded. Some two hundred other people were also injured, and a Turkish woman was killed. (Several weeks later a second U.S. serviceman, Staff Sergeant James E. Goins, died of wounds suffered in the bombing of La Belle discotheque.)

Immediately after the raid on Libya, U.S. president Ronald Reagan stated in a national telecast that, "the evidence is now conclusive that the terror bombing of La Belle discotheque was planned and executed under

Above: *Residents in Tripoli inspect the damage to their homes caused by the U.S. air strike of April 14, 1986. Below: a view of the destroyed interior of the La Belle discotheque in West Berlin.*

the direct orders of the Libyan regime." President Reagan had earlier warned Colonel Qaddafi that the United States would hold Qaddafi's regime responsible for any future terrorist attacks sponsored by Libya.

President Reagan did not say what the "conclusive evidence" was that had convinced him that Libya had participated in the Berlin terror bombing. However, later it was disclosed that a U.S. intelligence organization had intercepted telephone conversations between the terrorists in Berlin, discussing the bombing with their Libyan superiors. It was also reported that this information had been disclosed by the United States to the leaders of western European nations as well as to the U.S. Congress to convince them that drastic action was necessary. Apparently Britain's prime minister, Margaret Thatcher, was the only European leader sufficiently convinced by the evidence to allow her country to play even a minor role in the raid. There was no dissent from the U.S. Congress.

Public disclosure of the telephone intercepts by American intelligence sources was considered by some observers to be a breach of national security, since this made it clear not only to Libyans and Qaddafi but also to the Soviet Union that U.S. intelligence organizations were capable of performing such a feat. But it had long been fairly common knowledge in the world's intelligence community that the U.S. National Security Agency was engaged in such worldwide intercepts. Open disclosure of the Berlin-Libya telephone conversations, however, also made it clear that the U. S. had a working knowledge of whatever code the Libyans used for such messages, and this meant the Libyans would immediately introduce a new code that the Americans would have to break. But such intelligence problem-solving situations are more or less routine with the highly sophisticated U.S. intelligence organizations, and it is probable that any new code will be broken in a relatively short time.

EARLIER PROBLEMS
WITH QADDAFI

The bombing of Libya was actually the end result of a long series of provocative actions by the Qaddafi regime. As far back as December 1979, when Jimmy Carter was the U.S. president, a Libyan mob had destroyed the American embassy in Tripoli, Libya's capital city. This apparently was done to show Libya's sympathy and support for Iran's then newly installed leader, the Ayatollah Ruhollah Khomeini.

Khomeini's regime had begun when the shah of Iran, Mohammed Reza Pahlavi, was forced to feel that country and go into exile. A part of this exile was spent in the United States, where the shah underwent treatment for cancer. Khomeini demanded that the United States, which had long sponsored the shah's rule in Iran, return the shah to his homeland to stand trial. In an attempt to force the United States into giving in to Khomeini's demands, Iranian revolutionaries took over the American embassy in Teheran and held fifty-two Americans hostage.

Eighteen months after he had gone into exile, the shah of Iran died in an Egyptian military hospital in Cairo, at the age of sixty. Khomeini, however, continued to hold the Americans hostage in Iran. They were not released, in fact, until a few minutes after Ronald Reagan was inaugurated as the fortieth president of the United States on January 20, 1981. The fifty-two American hostages were held for 444 days. Most political observers were certain that the hostage situation in Iran was partly responsible for Carter's defeat by Reagan in his bid for reelection to the presidency.

The American public was also critical of Carter for his handling of the U.S.-Libyan situation. It was not until four months after the sacking of the U.S. embassy in Tripoli that Carter retaliated by expelling several Libyan diplomats from Washington, D.C., for threats they had made against anti-Qaddafi Libyan students studying in the United States. In addition, the Carter administration was embarrassed when it was learned that Billy Carter, the president's brother, had accepted a quarter of a million dollars in loans from the Qaddafi government. There was some question as to whether or not Billy Carter's ties to Libya should have required him to register as a foreign agent for that government.

QADDAFI AND
INTERNATIONAL TERRORISM

President Reagan came into office convinced that Qaddafi was not only a tool of the Soviet Union in the Middle East but also a power-hungry troublemaker who was bent on overthrowing pro-U.S. governments throughout Africa. In the spring of 1981 the Reagan administration ordered the closing of Libya's embassy in Washington, D.C., claiming that Libyan officials were giving support to international terrorists.

Reagan also strongly recommended that the fifteen hundred Americans living in Libya—most of them oil company employees and their families—leave that country as soon as possible. The U.S. State Department also prohibited all further travel by Americans to

Above: *the Ayatollah Khomeini, leader of Iran and its Muslim fundamentalists.* Below: *Shah Mohammed Reza Pahlavi and his wife, Empress Farah, leave Iran for a life in exile in the West.*

Libya. These moves were made at the urging of the National Security Council, the president said, to prevent a hostage situation like the one in Iran from developing in Libya. By March 1982, the number of Americans in Libya had been cut to fewer than four hundred. Those remaining had refused to leave.

Qaddafi scoffed at reports that he was linked to various bands of international terrorists, but there was strong circumstantial evidence that the Libyan dictator was indeed guilty of the charge. During 1980, all Libyans living abroad had been ordered to return to Libya. When a number of outspoken opponents of the regime did not, they were hunted down and killed. These assassinations by Libyan-sponsored "hit teams" took place in half a dozen European and Middle Eastern countries, and several such assassination attempts were reported in the United States.

Later, a British policewoman was killed by a shot fired by someone inside the Libyan embassy in London. This resulted in the expulsion of numerous Libyan diplomats from Great Britain and the closing of the Libyan embassy there, although the identity of the killer was never disclosed.

PLOT TO KILL
PRESIDENT REAGAN AND
OTHER U.S. OFFICIALS

Also in 1981 there were rumors in the American press and on television that a team of foreign assassins had been dispatched by Libya to kill President Reagan and other top American government officials. Whether or not these hit-team rumors were true, no chances were

Muammar Qaddafi giving a news conference in August 1983

taken. Security measures around the president and his aides were doubled.

President Reagan, who had already survived an assassination attempt by a disturbed young man named John Hinckley in March 1981, told the press he believed that the rumors were true. When Qaddafi denied them and called Reagan "silly and ignorant," Reagan countered with, "We have the evidence, and he knows it."

The exact nature of this evidence was not made public. Much of it apparently had been gathered by the U.S. Central Intelligence Agency (CIA) over a period of several months. The CIA also learned of a Libyan plot to kill the U.S. ambassador to Italy, Maxwell Rabb. Increased security measures apparently thwarted this effort. Then in November, an American State Department official, Christian Chapman, narrowly escaped assassination at the hands of unknown gunmen outside the U.S. embassy in Paris. This assault lent credence to widespread rumors that Qaddafi was out to kill U.S. State Department personnel throughout Europe. Later, the CIA observed Libyans spying on U.S. officials in Greece and Turkey. Again, increased protection appeared to forestall any additional assaults—at least temporarily. In response to all accusations that he was responsible for these incidents, Qaddafi continued to insist, "We refuse to assassinate any person."

But President Reagan and his National Security Council were not reassured. When told by reporters of Qaddafi's denials, Reagan commented, "If I were you, I wouldn't believe a word that man says."

QADDAFI'S "LINE OF DEATH" AT THE GULF OF SIDRA

On August 19, 1981, two U.S. Navy fighter aircraft were attacked by two Libyan jets over the Gulf of Sidra off

Two Libyan warplanes, Russian-built and thought to be similar to the one at the top of this picture, fired on two U.S. Navy F-14 jets similar to the one at the bottom of the picture.

the coast of Libya. A part of the U.S. Navy fleet was on maneuvers in this area; the American jets were flying protective cover for the warships. Qaddafi had long claimed that the Gulf of Sidra was a part of Libya's territorial waters, a claim that had never been recognized by any international body. Neither of the U.S. jets was damaged by the Libyan aerial attack, but in the ensuing dogfight the U.S. pilots shot down both Libyan planes.

Qaddafi's claims regarding the Gulf of Sidra continued to present a challenge to the United States and President Reagan for the next several years. The United States insisted that the main part of the Gulf was an international body of water through which the ships of all nations could sail freely. Qaddafi, however, drew what he called a "Line of Death" across the mouth of the gulf and declared that any warships that crossed this line would be destroyed by Libyan aircraft and shore batteries.

In March of 1986, just three weeks before American warplanes actually attacked Libya, the United States sent some elements of its Sixth Fleet directly into the Gulf of Sidra, challenging Qaddafi's so-called Line of Death. The Sixth Fleet's vessels sailing in the gulf were guarded by numerous carrier-based airplanes flying fighter cover.

Libya did not respond to this direct American challenge, although several radar-equipped Libyan communications vessels did approach the U.S. vessels. These small radar ships were promptly attacked by American planes and reportedly destroyed. A radar shore installation was also destroyed.

Tension between Libya and the United States continued to mount during the next several weeks, and rumors persisted that the United States was preparing an actual military attack of some kind against Qaddafi's troublesome North African nation. These rumors were confirmed with the U.S. Air Force and Navy bomb attack of April 14, 1986.

EUROPEAN AND U.S.
CIVILIAN REACTION TO
THE U.S. ATTACK

Immediately following the American attack on Libya there was strong public reaction against it by western Europeans. Britain's prime minister, Margaret Thatcher, was criticized both publicly and in Parliament for allowing some of the U.S. planes involved in the raid to take off from British airfields. On the continent, criticism was also widespread. Both France and Spain had refused to allow the American planes flying from Britain to use French and Spanish airspace, so the governments of these countries escaped public criticism from their own citizens.

In the United States, public opinion polls indicated general approval of the attack. However, there were some public demonstrations against it. There was also strong disapproval of France and Spain for forcing the U.S. F-111 bombers to take long detours around those countries on their way to and from Libya. Several weeks after the raid there was a report in one British paper, the Sunday *London Express*, that a French company was rebuilding and improving Libya's missile radar system, which had been destroyed by U.S. planes. This report caused additional criticism of the French by the American public, but French officials denied the *Express* story, saying it was "totally without foundation."

Interestingly, as the days and weeks passed following the raid, European criticism of the United States lessened considerably, and several European nations began to make moves to try to isolate Libya and Qaddafi. Meeting in Paris on April 17, twelve European

Community foreign ministers agreed to press ahead with antiterrorist measures. They identified Libya as "implicated in supporting terrorism," but they refused to close Libyan embassies in Europe—known as "people's bureaus"—as had been urged by President Reagan and Prime Minister Thatcher.

SUMMIT MEETING IN
JAPAN BACKS U.S.
ANTITERRORIST CAMPAIGN

Finally, early in May 1986, seven major nations held a summit meeting in Japan, and during the course of this meeting the seven nations branded Libya as a terrorist state. They also agreed to "make maximum efforts to combat terrorism relentlessly and without compromise." The seven nations signing this statement were the United States, Great Britain, Japan, France, Italy, West Germany, and Canada.

The summit meeting did not, however, call for any economic sanctions against Libya, which the United States favored. The United States was also disappointed when the other summit nations, especially Italy and West Germany, did not agree to cut back on purchases of oil from Libya. The U.S. position regarding oil purchases was weakened somewhat by the fact that there were still several American oil companies pumping oil in Libya despite the economic sanctions ordered by President Reagan earlier in 1986. The Reagan administration remedied this situation by refusing to renew beyond June 30 the licenses that allowed American oil companies to operate in Libya. The American companies complied with this ruling by selling off their Libyan oil holdings to foreign interests, which seemed only too eager to continue doing business in Libya. This was mainly because the oil from Libyan wells is of an

Summit leaders gather for lunch in Tokyo on May 5. From left to right they are: Jacques Delors of the European Community; Bettino Craxi of Italy; Rudolphus Lubbers of the European Community; Helmut Kohl of West Germany; Ronald Reagan of the United States; Yasuhiro Nakasone of Japan; François Mitterrand of France; Margaret Thatcher of Great Britain; and Brian Mulroney of Canada.

extremely high grade that is ideal for refining into gasoline.

TERRORISM CAUSES CUTBACK IN EUROPEAN TRAVEL

Much of the reason for the European nations signing the summit antiterrorism pledge in Japan was purely a matter of self-interest. If terrorist attacks continued, Europe would lose billions of dollars from tourist travel as Americans decided to take their vacations in the United States or in areas of the world where terrorism was not so apt to occur. Already in 1986, airlines, hotels, and travel agencies were experiencing massive cancellations of reservations made earlier by Americans who planned to travel in Europe.

After the American raid on Libya many American students were among those who changed their vacation plans. According to Michael I. Eizenberg, president of the American Council for International Studies, a hundred thousand American students travel to Europe each year on school-related trips. About half of those scheduled to travel in the summer of 1986 changed their plans, Eizenberg reported.

Libya, of course, was not the only nation guilty of exporting terrorism. Syria and Iran as well as radical Muslim groups throughout the MIddle East had made 1985 a banner year for international terrorist activity. In June a TWA passenger jet had been hijacked by Shiite Muslims and its passengers and crew temporarily held hostage. In October an Italian cruise liner, the *Achille Lauro*, had been hijacked by terrorists belonging to the Palestine Liberation Organization (PLO). There had also been murderous attacks by unknown assassins in the airports of Rome and Vienna.

Each time one of these attacks occurred, an accusing finger was immediately pointed at Libya and Qaddafi. But accusatory fingers could just as easily have been

The Achille Lauro *docks in Genoa, Italy, and prepares for another cruise after the terrorist hijacking of October 1986.*

PLO chief Yasser Arafat

pointed at Khomeini in Iran, President Hafez Assad in Syria, and Yasser Arafat of the PLO. In fact, as the investigation of the bombing of La Belle discotheque in Germany continued, there were strong indications that Syrians as well as Libyans had been involved.

QADDAFI ACCUSED OF
BUYING HOSTAGES

In the spring and summer of 1986 Qaddafi was accused of having bought and then executing one American and two Britons who had been held hostage in Lebanon. These unfortunate victims were just three of upwards of a dozen Western-world hostages who had been held captive in Lebanon for as long as several years.

The suspicion that Qaddafi was actually trying to buy U.S. hostages from their Lebanese captors was first raised by *Time* and *Newsweek* magazines in April. Then in August, California congressman Robert K. Dornan openly accused Qaddafi of having bought U.S. hostage Peter Kilburn and Britain's Leigh Douglas and Philip Padfield from Arab revolutionaries. The three hostages had been found dead on April 17 in Lebanon. Dornan also said that Qaddafi had wanted to do the same to all U.S. hostages in Lebanon but had failed. U.S. officials refused to either confirm or deny these reports.

LIBYAN REACTIONS TO
THE AMERICAN BOMBING

Qaddafi, of course, continued to claim complete innocence of any and all terrorist activities. This was an obvious lie, but he repeated it to his people following the American air raid on Tripoli and Benghazi in mid-April 1986.

He also lashed out at the Western nations, especially the United States and President Reagan and Britain and Prime Minister Thatcher, and promised retaliation against them. His most immediate form of retaliation took an academic rather than a military turn. He abolished English as Libya's second language after Arabic. This move put out of work thousands of teachers of English, most of whom had been recruited from Ghana. It caused a considerable amount of unrest not only among the teachers but also among Libyan students who had wanted to learn English as a means of gaining employment in western Europe.

But the most serious unrest was caused by the simple fact that Libya had actually been bombed, plus the threat of possible future bombings. Qaddafi had always assured his people that no Western nation would dare attack Libya, for fear of instant and massive retaliation by Libya and its powerful ally, the Soviet Union. But no such retaliation was forthcoming. The Soviet Union strongly protested the American attack but took no further action. For some months, in fact, the Soviets had indicated a growing disenchantment with the unpredictable, unreliable Colonel Qaddafi.

Qaddafi himself also seemed shocked and somewhat dazed by the American attack. For several days after the bombing he remained in hiding, giving rise to speculation that he had been killed. When he did reappear he spoke from an isolated television studio at a secret location. As was expected he spoke about the "demons of the West," who had attacked his country and killed innocent civilians, including his adopted daughter.

But Western diplomats all agreed that Qaddafi's heart did not seem to be in his denunciation of the West. The Libyan leader's protests were also somewhat weakened by the fact that there was considerable doubt that Qaddafi even had an adopted daughter. A former Libyan prime minister, Abdel-Hamid Bakoush, currently in exile in Egypt, insisted that the report that Qaddafi's "adopted daughter" was one of the casualties was a lie. "Qaddafi never had an adopted daughter," Bakoush said. "He just made up that story to convince Libyans he was sharing in their grief."

During the course of the next few months Qaddafi made several more televised public speeches, but all of them continued to seem disoriented, incoherent ramblings. Qaddafi acted as if he were suffering from severe depression or was perhaps drugged.

Soon rumors began to circulate that Qaddafi was no longer the all-powerful dictator of Libya. These rumors grew when an attempt by unidentified assassins was made on the life of Qaddafi's second-in-command,

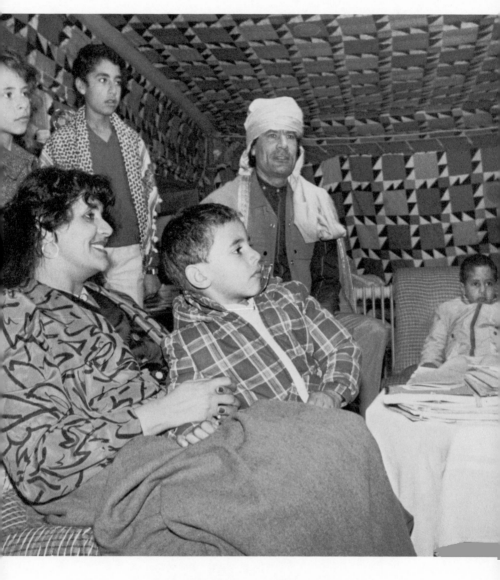

Qaddafi, his wife, Safia, and
four of their seven children in a
tent on the outskirts of Tripoli

Major Abdul Salaam Jalloud, in mid-May. Jalloud escaped the assassination attempt near his home in Tripoli, but it was rumored that the attempt was part of an army coup to kill off several top Libyan leaders, including Qaddafi, following which a quartet of military men would take over the government.

Whatever truth there was to the rumors, Qaddafi made all attempts on his life just about impossible by ruling from a roving headquarters on board a luxurious armored bus, which had originally been built for him by the West German automobile manufacturer Mercedes. Accompanying the armored bus was a platoon of bodyguards in armored vehicles.

Whether or not Qaddafi's fortunes are on the decline is purely a matter of speculation. Some of the talk about it may well have been the result of wishful thinking on the part of Western leaders. No one, however, is ready to predict the colorful Colonel Qaddafi's downfall. Too often in the past he has been down and all but counted out, only to arise, more powerful than ever, as the leader of the Libyan people.

TWO

WHO IS QADDAFI?

Had President Reagan and his administration over-reacted in bombing Libya? Some skeptics said that a superpower such as the United States, with its 240 million people, attacking a tiny North African desert nation such as Libya, with its 3.5 million people, was like using a sledgehammer to kill a fly.

Why had President Reagan reacted so violently against Qaddafi? Who is this mercurial desert dictator who can provoke anger from the mightiest nation in the Free World?

Muammar Qaddafi is the son of a nomad farmer and cattle trader. His family name is spelled in a variety of ways in various English-language publications—Qaddafi, Gaddafi, Qadhafi, Kaddafi, Khadafy, el-Qaddafi, and al-Gadafy. His given name is also spelled in a variety of ways—Muammar, Mu'ammar, Muammer, and Moammar, for example. None of these spellings is necessarily wrong, and all are to some degree correct. Actually, there is no one correct way to translate the Libyan dictator's name from the Arabic language into English. Each rendering is an attempt to do so phonetically, to make it sound in English as it does in Arabic.

Qaddafi was born in 1942 in a tent in Libya's Fazzan Desert region near the coastal town of Sirte. This was during World War II, when Libya was under the control of Italy's Fascist government, headed by the dictator Benito Mussolini. While Qaddafi was still an infant, warfare raged across his country as the Italian armies, aided by their German allies, the Nazis, tried to defend Libya against the attacking British military forces.

Before World War II ended, the Italians and Germans were driven out of Libya as well as the whole of North Africa by the British and their allies, the Americans. Neither Qaddafi's parents nor relatives, nor any other Libyan Arabs for that matter, were sorry to see the Italians and Germans go. Qaddafi later recalled that even as a child, he and all other Arabs were treated like dogs by the Fascists and the Nazis. This treatment wounded his pride. His tribal upbringing and education in strict Muslim schools, however, gave him a strong sense of being Arab in general and Libyan in particular. Qaddafi's powerful belief in Arab nationalism has been a driving force behind his actions since he was a boy.

Qaddafi spent much of his boyhood in the Fazzan Desert. It was a Spartan life, with no luxuries. But it was a life the boy loved, and it is still much a part of him. Even in his adulthood, Qaddafi has from time to time returned to a tent in the desert for periods of silent meditation and study of the Koran, the holy book of the Muslims. It was in similar surroundings as a boy that he sat silently listening to the tribal elders talk of the Arab dream—the establishment of an Arabian Islamic state (Islam is Libya's official state religion) across the whole of Saharan North Africa. This had been a goal of Libyan leaders since early in the nineteenth century.

THE YOUNG NATIONALIST

In Muammar Qaddafi's mind, the dream of Arab nationalism grew and prospered. One of his early idols was

Gamal Abdel Nasser, then president of Egypt. Nasser, too, was a fervent Arab nationalist. From Cairo, Nasser's regular radio broadcasts, *Voice of the Arabs*, preached nationalism and were listened to religiously by young Qaddafi and other patriotic students attending secondary schools in Tripoli.

When he was just fourteen, young Qaddafi organized a student strike at his school in support of Nasser against the British, who then controlled Egypt's Suez Canal. Qaddafi was temporarily expelled for starting this strike, but his revolutionary ardor was not cooled. Later he returned to secondary school, graduated, and went on to briefly attend Libya's University of Benghazi and then the Libyan military academy.

Following his graduation from the military academy, Qaddafi was sent to Great Britain's Royal Army Signal School near London. Few Arabs studying abroad wore their native dress in those days, but to show his pride as an Arab, Qaddafi always wore his. In London, his Arab headdress and flowing robes often stopped traffic as Qaddafi paraded proudly through the streets.

Qaddafi returned to Libya as an army captain. After the expulsion of the Italians and Germans from Libya during World War II, the country had come under British and French control. But after the war ended, the United Nations, the newly formed international peacekeeping organization set up by the victorious western Allies, decreed that Libya should be allowed to become an independent kingdom. The head of this kingdom was to be Mohammed Idris Al-Sanusi, commonly called King Idris. Qaddafi served loyally under King Idris for several years, receiving regular promotions until he attained the rank of major.

But Qaddafi and several of his fellow officers were dissatisfied with King Idris's reign, partly because Idris was only lukewarm on the subject of Arab nationalism. The Idris regime was also quite corrupt, and much of the opposition he faced grew out of that. In addition, oil

King Idris Al-Sanusi of Libya in 1955
Facing page: *President Nasser of Egypt meets with Nikita Khrushchev, leader of the Soviet Union, at the Russian Consulate in New York in 1960.*

had been discovered in the Libyan desert in 1959, and soon the nation's earnings skyrocketed. Qaddafi and his fellow officers did not think that enough of this money was being spent on building up Libya's military strength so that the nation could be totally free from the threat of outside control.

On September 1, 1969, King Idris was deposed in a bloodless military coup. Twelve of the officers who took part in the coup then formed a Revolutionary Command Council to rule the country. This Council was to be assisted by a civilian cabinet that would help run Libya "democratically." But it soon became clear that a military dictatorship had been established in Libya and that Qaddafi, who promoted himself to the rank of colonel, was the strongman in this dictatorship.

In light of Qaddafi's later difficulties with the United States, it is interesting to note that he probably never could have come into power if the United States had opposed his revolution against King Idris. But at that time Qaddafi was freely expressing strong anti-Russian sentiments. Since the United States wanted to keep Soviet influence out of the Middle East, a strong anti-Soviet government in Libya—even if it was a dictatorship—seemed worthy of support.

The United States maintained cordial relations with Libya for several years despite the fact that soon after he took control Qaddafi ordered the elimination of all foreign military bases in Libya, including an American air base outside Tripoli. The United States accepted Qaddafi's move as a legitimate effort to free Libya from all foreign influence. So cordial did these relations remain, in fact, that the U.S. Central Intelligence Agency is said to have warned Qaddafi of an attempted coup against his regime in 1971.

But in 1973, following a brief war between Israel and Egypt (assisted by Syria), Egypt began working with the United States to gain acceptance of Israel

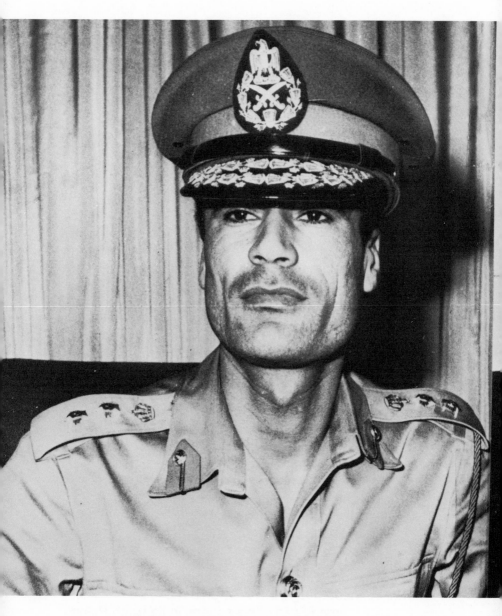

*Qaddafi, at 28, becomes one of the
youngest heads of state in the world.*

among the Arab nations of the Middle East. This angered Qaddafi, who has never wavered in his anti-Israel attitude, and he soon began to make overtures toward the Soviet Union.

Over the next several years, Qaddafi bought well over $12 billion worth of military equipment from the Russians, including tanks, aircraft, artillery, and other combat hardware. Soon there were Soviet military advisers stationed in Libya, teaching Qaddafi's army and air force how to use this equipment. By the time President Reagan took office, these advisers numbered several thousand. Their presence was one of the reasons Reagan reacted so strongly at first to Qaddafi's anti-American moves. Borrowing from an old Arab proverb, the president pointed out that if a camel were allowed to get his nose under the tent, soon the whole camel would be inside. Reagan saw the Russian military advisers as the camel's nose.

But his fears were not to be realized. Although Qaddafi had taken to calling the Soviet Union a friend and the United States a "devil," he continued to flatly refuse to allow any foreign military bases in his country—including those of the Soviet Union. Several observers pointed out that the Russians didn't know how to deal with Qaddafi any better than the Americans did.

THE POLISH CONNECTION

Qaddafi, however, continued to maintain close military ties with the Soviet Union and Soviet-controlled countries. Early in 1982 several hundred young Libyan army cadets were flown to Warsaw, Poland, for special military training. This special-weapons training program was sponsored by the Soviet Union.

Libya already had close economic ties with Poland before a political crisis occurred there in late 1981 and martial law was imposed by the Polish Communist military government on December 13. Some fourteen thousand Polish citizens were already working in Libya, on construction projects, road building, and communications installations, and there was limited trade between the two countries. During the Polish crisis, Qaddafi was one of the first national leaders outside the bloc of Communist nations to express support of the military takeover in Poland. Qaddafi also accused the Reagan administration of launching "a frontal attack against the forces of progress and independence" in Poland.

Polish leaders attempted to exploit Qaddafi's support by expanding Polish-Libyan trade and doubling the number of Poles working in Libya. In return, Poland hoped to get for itself favorable oil deals, since it imports 30 percent of its oil from Arab countries.

WHAT DOES QADDAFI WANT?

Today there is little doubt in most Western observers' minds that Qaddafi is very much his own person, taking orders from no one and wanting only what he believes best for his country. This, of course, can be an admirable quality. But it can have a dark side as well. Adolf Hitler was also his own person and a fierce nationalist, but the methods he used to attain his goals resulted not only in the deaths of millions of European Jews and others but also in World War II, the costliest war in history in terms of human lives and property damage. Unfortunately, Qaddafi's methods have at times resembled Hitler's. Qaddafi, of course, has never attempted the wholesale slaughter of Jews, as did Hitler, but he has never been willing to admit the right of Israel to exist as a nation. Given the opportunity, there is little doubt that Qaddafi would expel both Israel and the Jews from the Middle East.

Qaddafi regards himself as Nasser's true successor in the Middle East. Like the former Egyptian presi-

Qaddafi meets with President Anwar Sadat (left)
of Egypt and President Hafez Assad of Syria to form
a loose alliance of Arab republics in April 1971.

dent, Gamal Abdel Nasser, he dreams of a pan-Arab nation stretching from Senegal to the Sudan. He also dreams, of course, of becoming the ruler of such a Saharan Islamic republic. But every time Qaddafi has taken any step to establish such a republic, he has been halted in his tracks. Consequently, he is a frustrated man.

"My problem is," Qaddafi has said, "I have no such country to lead, though I am a great leader."

During the early years of his rule in the 1970s, Qaddafi tried to convince Tunisia, Egypt, and Syria that they should merge with Libya to form a Confederation of Arab Republics. The negotiations with Tunisia and Egypt never got much past the opening stages. Syria did technically merge with Libya, but this was nothing more than a symbolic gesture.

Late in 1980, Qaddafi tried to force a new merger. He sent Libyan troops into neighboring Chad, where there was a civil war taking place. The troops, Qaddafi said at first, were sent in to give support to Chad's president, Goukouni Woddei. But soon, Qaddafi declared that Libya and Chad had merged and that he was keeping some ten thousand Libyan troops in Chad to enforce this merger. Both the United Nations and the Organization of African Unity demanded that Qaddafi remove this occupation force. The Libyan dictator reluctantly complied, but no one knew just how long he would continue to do so. Qaddafi's plans had long included not only Chad but also sections of Niger and Algeria as part of what he called "Greater Libya."

Qaddafi's interest in Chad was more than political. The Libyan dictator has long wanted to add nuclear weapons to his country's arsenal, and Chad is believed to be rich in uranium, an essential ingredient in the production of nuclear explosives.

Frustrated in fulfilling his dreams of restoring pride to Libya and the other Arab nations, Qaddafi has sometimes resorted to terrorist tactics. When Egypt's President Nasser died in 1970, he was succeeded by one of his aides, Anwar el-Sadat. For a time, Qaddafi was as friendly with Sadat as he had been with Nasser. This friendship was based on two things—Sadat's efforts to establish a United Arab Republic and his professed determination to destroy Israel. Like his predecessor, Sadat even waged war against the Israeli nation. But when Sadat changed his position and began to make overtures of peace and friendship toward Israel, Qaddafi turned against the Egyptian president. He did not think Israel had the right to exist as a nation, and he opposed any Arab leader who did think so—even if this meant continual warfare in the Middle East.

THE ISRAELI QUESTION

Hebrew or Jewish tribes had lived since ancient times in the area of the Middle East known as Palestine. In fact, the Jews had established an important early civilization there. But they were driven out by the Romans and scattered throughout Europe and the Middle East. For centuries they had no true homeland.

Then in the late nineteenth century, a group of European Jews calling themselves Zionists made a serious attempt to reestablish a Jewish homeland in Palestine. The group took their name from the Hill of Zion, in the ancient Jewish capital and holy city of Jerusalem. This Zionist pioneering movement was to lead to the eventual creation of the State of Israel.

During World War I, there was fighting throughout the Middle East, and British troops, aided by some of the Palestinian Jews, occupied Palestine. Near the end of the war, a British scientist and later Israeli statesman named Chaim Weizmann persuaded the British government to issue an official statement in behalf of the establishment of Palestine as a Jewish national homeland. This statement was called the Balfour Declaration.

After World War I ended, an international peacekeeping organization called the League of Nations was established. The League approved the Balfour Declaration, and in 1922 Great Britain was named by the League to rule Palestine under a mandate arrangement. In other words, Britain, under the overall authority of the League of Nations, was expected to prepare its mandated territory for self-government.

After Palestine became a mandated territory many thousands of Jews moved there. But by this time the Arabs in Palestine had also become nationalistic. They wanted Palestine to become an Arab state, not a new Jewish one. Conflict broke out between the Arabs and Jews that lasted right up to the eve of World War II in 1939.

During this prewar period many Jews were driven out of Germany by the Nazis, and some of these refugees fled to Palestine. The Arabs resented the intrusion of these additional Jews and carried on guerrilla warfare against them. Britain, apparently unable to stop this fighting, yielded to Arab demands and virtually ended further Jewish immigration into Palestine. The Jews strongly protested Britain's action.

During World War II, a solution to the problem was postponed. But after the war, the problem again became acute. When Britain's mandate over Palestine ended in 1947, it turned the Palestinian problem over to the new world peacekeeping organization, the United Nations. The United Nations' solution was simple. It proposed that Palestine be split into two independent states, one Arab, the other Jewish. The Arabs protested strongly against the proposal, but it was eagerly accepted by the Jews. Under the auspices of the United Nations, the independent State of Israel was established by proclamation on May 14, 1948.

A British peacekeeping military force remained in the area until the new state could actually be organized. But when the British troops left, Israel's neighboring Arab states attacked and tried to destroy the new Jewish homeland.

By the end of 1948, when the United Nations was able to end most of the fighting in the area, Israel still existed. The United States was the first country to formally recognize it. With financial and military aid from Western nations, principally the United States, and financial aid from Jews throughout the world, the new nation on the western edge of Asia had managed to survive its baptism by fire.

But sporadic attacks against Israel continued. One of the main aggressors was Egypt. First under Nasser in 1967 and then under Sadat in 1973, Egypt waged all-out war against the Israelis. Despite the fact that Egypt was joined by Syrian, Jordanian, Lebanese, and other pro-Arab Palestinian Liberation Organization (PLO) military forces, the Israelis were victorious in both of these conflicts as well as in numerous other border clashes.

Despite powerful peace efforts brought to bear by both the United States and the United Nations, the continued conflict between the Arabs and Jews threatened not only the stability of the Middle East region but also world peace. Then, in 1976, a remarkable event occurred. President Anwar Sadat, who had been pro-Hitler in World War II, gradually swung over to the view that the Jews had a right to their homeland and that war between Arabs and Jews should cease. Sadat's motives were not entirely altruistic. The Egyptian leader was a practical man who thought that peace would be in the best interests of the Arabs as well as the Jews. He had also learned—the hard way—that the Israelis were formidable foes in war.

President Sadat undertook to go to Israel in mid-

President Anwar Sadat of Egypt (left) and President Jimmy Carter (center) shakes hands with Prime Minister Menachem Begin of Israel at Camp David in March 1979.

1977 with a peace initiative. He did so at great risk to his own life—not at the hands of the Israelis but at the hands of Arabs who refused to recognize the State of Israel's right to exist. U.S. president Jimmy Carter immediately seized upon Sadat's peace initiative and began one of his own. He invited President Sadat and Israel's prime minister, Menachem Begin, to Washington for a peace conference.

Carter, Sadat, and Begin met at Camp David, the presidential retreat near Washington, in September 1978. Here, after lengthy and difficult negotiations, Egypt and Israel agreed on a framework for peace in the Middle East. A treaty between the two countries, called the Camp David Peace Accords, was signed in Washington on March 26, 1979.

Meanwhile, Libya's Muammar Qaddafi had come to regard Sadat as a traitor to the Arab cause. No sooner had Sadat in 1976 and 1977 taken his first steps to establish peace than Qaddafi set out to sabotage them. According to U.S. intelligence sources, Qaddafi hired two Egyptian expatriates to assassinate the American ambassador to Egypt, Hermann F. Eilts. This assassination, Qaddafi believed, would disrupt U.S.-Egyptian relations and end any Egyptian peace-making efforts with Israel.

The two-man hit team sponsored by Qaddafi was hired by a Venezuelan terrorist who went by the name of Carlos and was nicknamed "The Jackal." (Carlos's real name is Ilyich Ramirez Sanchez.) According to intelligence reports, Carlos worked for Qaddafi. The assassination attempt was canceled, however, when one of the two hit men was captured and divulged details of the plot.

When evidence of the conspiracy was turned over to then-President Jimmy Carter, Carter decided to send a private warning to Qaddafi. Although Qaddafi stoutly denied involvement in the plot and demanded to see the evidence, Carter's confrontation with the Libyan dictator ended that particular assassination conspiracy.

Even before Reagan assumed the presidency, he was fully briefed on all of Qaddafi's terrorist activities. Thus, when Reagan became president and evidence began to mount that Qaddafi was out to renew his assassination attempts against American officials, Reagan may have decided that the best way to nip such plots in the bud was to confront Qaddafi with them just as President Carter had done earlier.

The Reagan administration was concerned also over reports that Qaddafi might be teaching terrorist tactics in place of diplomacy to the leaders of other small, third-world countries for use against the major powers. There were many rumors that Qaddafi had established in Libya a school for terrorists headed by some former members of the CIA, by some ex–Army Special Forces soldiers (Green Berets), who had learned methods of guerrilla warfare while fighting in Vietnam, and by other soldiers of fortune. All of these expatriates were said to have sold their services to Qaddafi purely for the huge salaries he offered them. If terrorism ever did succeed in replacing diplomacy and the terrorists were to obtain nuclear weapons, then the real possibility of a complete breakdown in international relations could not be ignored.

THE TERM "ASSASSIN" ORIGINATED IN THE MIDDLE EAST

If Qaddafi's school for terrorist assassins does indeed exist, it is not the first such school in the Middle East. In fact, the term *assassin* has a long and infamous history there, dating back to the eleventh century. At that time a Muslim named Hassan ben Sabah established a secret religious sect in Persia (today's Iran) whose followers killed their enemies not by fighting them in open battle but by secretly murdering them.

Hassan ben Sabah maintained the loyalty of his followers, all of whom he taught the skills of murder by stealth, by supplying them with the drug hashish. Made from Indian hemp, hashish is similar to today's widely used marijuana, or "pot." This use of hashish gave the members of this murderous sect their name—the *Hashishins*, or "Assassins."

For two centuries, the Assassins under various leaders spread the terror of their name from Iran to Egypt. In the twelfth century, they moved their headquarters to Syria, where they successfully plotted to secretly kill several European leaders. Early in the century, however, they began to kill one another in a civil war over the sect's leadership. Finally their enemies banded together to stamp them out. Twelve thousand Assassins were massacred before the sect died out in 1256. Some of the Assassins' practices, unfortunately, have carried over to the present day.

PEACE IN THE MIDDLE EAST IS STILL THREATENED

On October 6, 1981, less than nine months after President Reagan's inauguration, Anwar Sadat was assassinated in Cairo. The assassins were Islamic fundamentalists who were fanatically opposed to Sadat's dealings with Israel. There was no indication that Qaddafi had either engineered or been in any way involved in Sadat's murder, but he applauded the deed nonetheless.

Sadat was succeeded in office by his close aide, Hosni Mubarak. Mubarak was a man as dedicated to peace in the Middle East as his predecessor had been. One of his first acts upon taking office was to pledge to live up to the Camp David Accords. It was not immediately clear, however, whether he was secure enough in his own country to become as powerful a leader in the Middle East as Sadat had been.

Obviously, one of the troublemakers Mubarak would have to deal with was Qaddafi. With Sadat no longer in power, Qaddafi might well renew his attempts to become the Middle East's strongman. Signs of such efforts began to appear soon after Mubarak became president. Qaddafi sent Libyan bombers into neighbor-

Hosni Mubarak being sworn in as Egypt's new president, following the assassination of Anwar Sadat

ing Sudan as a sign of support to dissident Sudanese who were trying to overthrow their president, Gaafar Nimeiry. Nimeiry had been a close ally of Sadat, and thus an enemy of Qaddafi. In response, Nimeiry called on both the United States and Egypt for assistance in "physically liquidating" his "tormentor," Qaddafi. Egypt responded by sending antiaircraft units to the Sudan.

Qaddafi also stirred up trouble by sending terrorists into Egypt to set off bombs at the airport in Cairo. Following this incident, President Mubarak declared a state of emergency along the Egyptian-Libyan border. Once before, there had been a brief border encounter between Egyptian and Libyan armies. This was when Sadat had first begun to make overtures of peace toward Israel. In that brief clash, the Libyans had come off a sad second best, and when Sadat was asked why Qaddafi had started such an apparently senseless military action, Sadat had replied, "I don't know why. What I do know is that Qaddafi is a certified lunatic."

This time, there was no actual clash between Libyan and Egyptian forces, but the threat of such action still remains a real one. And, lunatic or not, Qaddafi's possible future actions are serious and justifiable cause for worry among world leaders. For, although to many observers he may seem like the insignificant leader of an insignificant country, it was also an apparently insignificant man, Gavrilo Princip, in the apparently insignificant Balkan country of Bosnia, who assassinated Austria-Hungary's Archduke Francis Ferdinand in 1914 and thus triggered World War I. Like the Balkans in 1914, the Middle East in the mid-1980s is a powder keg that any chance spark might explode into another world war. Qaddafi's terrorist activities and his support of assassination plots such as those against innocent civilians and officials of foreign governments could easily be that spark.

THREE

THE LAND AND THE PEOPLE OF THE SOCIALIST PEOPLE'S LIBYAN ARAB JAMAHIRIYA

Even before the United States bombed Libya in the spring of 1986, Qaddafi's popularity had begun to decline among the Libyan people. Living standards, which had improved dramatically in the 1970s, once again began to decline in the mid-1980s. Annual per capita income, which had soared from $1,700 to $9,000 in the early years of the Qaddafi regime, suddenly sank to near poverty levels.

The decline in living standards was partly due to bad domestic economic policy. Mainly, however, the decline was due to the worldwide oil glut, which caused Libya's income to plummet drastically.

Libya's domestic economy was badly damaged by Qaddafi's efforts to ensure the economic equality of all Libyans. To accomplish this, Qaddafi put into effect radical measures. All retail trade was abolished, and the government seized private bank accounts as well as privately operated businesses. As a result, private investment came to a standstill and shortages of consumer goods were widespread. Soon a vast black market sprang up, in which people illegally bought goods from illegal dealers. Today, virtually all Libyan families are involved in the corrupt black market in order to survive.

Agricultural production has also dropped severely due to the government overemphasis on mechanization. Indiscriminate mechanization has led to unneeded irrigation, which has so depleted the country's scanty underground water supply that future cultivation is in jeopardy.

To make up for the losses from private investment, the government has attempted to make its own investments in major industry. But outside the petroleum industry there has been little major industrial development. This is partly due to the government's unrealistic wage, price, and employment policies. As Middle East expert Lisa Anderson has pointed out in the *Middle East Journal*, spring 1986: "Perhaps 75 per cent of the Libyan labor force is in the 'public' sector, drawing salaries for appearing at the office, while foreign nationals staff more than half the managerial and professional positions in the economy." Bureaucracy, like the black market, has become a way of Libyan life. Both are severely damaging to the economy.

Despite all of these problems, however, Libya remains an extremely wealthy country, especially compared with other Third World nonindustrial nations of the world. Libya's affluence is primarily based on two things: its abundance of oil and its key location in the Mediterranean Sea.

LOCATION, SIZE, POPULATION, AND MAJOR CITIES

Libya is one of a group of five North African nations bordering the southern Mediterranean. They are, from west to east, Morocco, Algeria, Tunisia, Libya, and Egypt. Libya's northern border along the Mediterra-

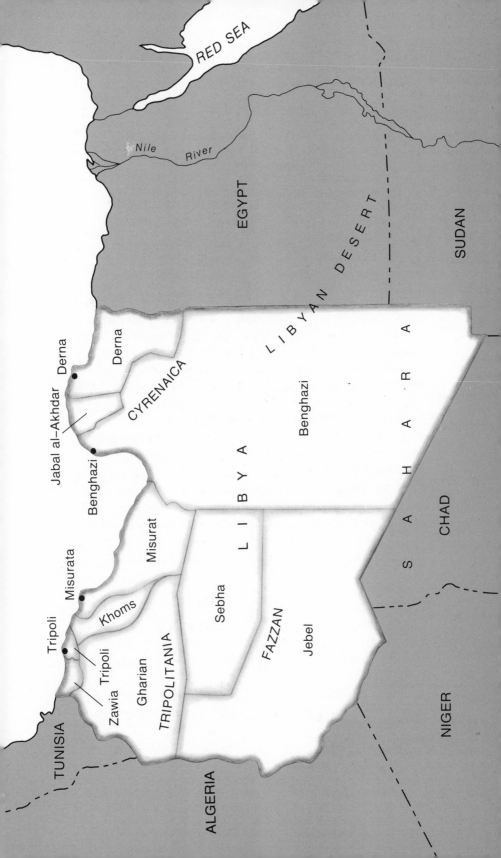

nean extends for about a thousand miles (1,600 km). To the west, Libya is bordered by Algeria and Tunisia. To the south, it is bordered by Niger and Chad. To the southeast lies a small border portion of the Sudan, and to the east is a lengthy border with Egypt.

Libya's location and sheer size give it major strategic advantages in its possible future political role in Africa. Its area is 679,358 square miles (1,759,537 sq. km), making it larger than Alaska and the six New England states of the United States combined. The country is divided into ten provinces, which are similar to American states: Tripoli, Benghazi, Sebha, Zawia, Khoms, Misurata, Derna, Jebel, Akhdar, and Gharian. Its three major regions are Tripolitania, Cyrenaica, and Fazzan.

Libya has a population of approximately 3.5 million, most of whom live along the Mediterranean coast. Inland there is mainly desert or semidesert, which makes up some 95 percent of the country. Most of the people are Arabs and Berbers, although there is also a small foreign population, mostly European.

The country's largest cities are its capital, Tripoli, with a population of about 858,500, Benghazi (population 420,000), and Misurata (population 250,000). All three of these cities are situated on the Mediterranean and are important seaports from which oil and other export products are shipped. Derna is an important city in U.S. history (see Chapter IV). Also situated on the Mediterranean, it has a population of about 60,000.

MAJOR EXPORTS

Crude petroleum, or crude oil, makes up 99 percent of Libya's export products. Other exports include barley, wheat, olives, dates, figs, tomatoes, almonds, and citrus fruits.

Libya produced about 750,000 barrels of oil a day during the early 1980s, ranking it fifteenth in world pro-

Above: *a view of the city of Tripoli, near the docks, in Libya.* Below: *an oil well in Libya's Cyrenaica province*

duction. This brought the country a revenue of some $15 billion annually. In the mid 1980s, however, there was a worldwide oil glut, and Libya's production and income were cut in half.

LANGUAGES, RELIGION, AND EDUCATION

The official language of Libya is Arabic, although there are still some Berber-speaking people living in villages in the desert. Virtually all Libyan Arabs, including Qaddafi, rigidly follow Sunni-Muslim religious customs. Alcohol is forbidden, and it is illegal even for tourists to bring it into the country. Smoking is frowned upon, as are most forms of commercial entertainment, although these bans have been somewhat relaxed in recent years. During the 1980s, in fact, literally millions of transistor radios were imported into the country, enough to supply each Libyan with nine radios apiece.

There is compulsory education through the elementary grades, and Qaddafi's government has provided universal free education up through the university level. More than ten thousand students attend the University of Libya at Benghazi, which also has a branch at Tripoli. The curriculum includes the fine arts, teaching methods, economics, and petroleum engineering. Many young Libyans also study abroad at foreign universities. Also, in Tripoli there is an elementary school for non-Libyan students whose parents work for the various foreign oil companies operating in Libya. American teachers and students in this school were forced to return home or find jobs elsewhere overseas during the continuing U.S.-Libyan crisis of the mid-1980s.

THE IMPORTANCE OF CLIMATE

Like most of the rest of northern Africa, Libya is separated from southern Africa by the Sahara Desert, which

*The desert spring of Brak, one of
the many lush oases that exist in Libya*

stretches from the Atlantic Ocean to the Red Sea. In
Libya, a part of the Sahara's vast, sandy wastes are
known as the Libyan, or Fazzan, Desert; this is the area
where Qaddafi was born. Here the temperature has
been known to reach 136°F (58°C), one of the highest
temperatures ever recorded on earth.

Lack of water is a problem throughout Libya. There
are no permanent rivers or lakes. Average annual rainfall at Tripoli is only 13 inches (33 cm), and in the desert
it is far less. Every few years there are severe droughts
that damage crops even along the fertile Mediterranean
coast. Most Libyan farmers wish that water rather than
oil was the abundant resource in their country.

Another disagreeable feature of the Libyan climate
is the so-called *ghibli.* This is a hot, dry, dust-laden
southern wind that blows for as long as a week. Occur-

ring in the spring and fall, the *ghibli* causes the temperature to rise as much as 50°F (10°C) in only a few hours. A similar phenomenon, known as a *chinook*, occurs in the spring in the Pacific Northwest and Rocky Mountain regions of the United States.

Climatic conditions along the Mediterranean coast are relatively moderate, although during the summer temperatures there reach the high nineties (36° or 37°C), with the humidity as high as 90 percent. Because of the extreme weather conditions in the Libyan desert regions, 90 percent of the people live in less than 10 percent of the country's total area, mainly along the coast. Most of the desert-dwellers cluster around the numerous oases, many of which have been created by sinking deep wells into the water table that underlies much of Libya. Some of these oases are among the richest in northern Africa and produce dates, figs, grain, and citrus fruits.

DISCOVERY OF "BLACK GOLD" CHANGES DESERT LIFESTYLE

Since the discovery of "black gold" in the Libyan desert region in 1959, a whole new desert life-style has emerged. Within two years after it was discovered, oil was being produced and exported. Pipelines were built in record time to carry the oil from the desert oil fields to Libya's seaports. As the oil flowed out, enormous riches began to flow in. Some of these riches were used to improve the living and working conditions in the oil fields.

In the beginning, much of Libya's oil industry was owned by foreign nations—the Netherlands, Great Britain, France, Italy, and the United States. But under Qaddafi's dictatorship, Libya soon began to nationalize its oil industry, gradually taking over control from the foreign companies. Libya still needs outside engineers and technicians to run this highly complex industry, but more and more of the workers—the manual laborers and drilling crews—are Libyans. As a result, it has been Libyans who have benefited most from the improved oil-field conditions.

Salaries were the first thing to improve. Libyan oil-field laborers earned more in a month than they formerly earned in a year as farmers or city workers. Living and working conditions improved rapidly, too. The oil camps were turned into cool oases in the heart of the vast desert. Air-conditioned trailer houses were provided for the oil crews, who often had their families living with them. There were also indoor swimming pools and, in the evening, movies. Experienced cooks were hired to prepare food flown in from Tripoli.

At first there were few vacations or paid holidays for oil-field workers, including those from foreign countries. American and European workers, however, objected to such a Spartan routine—despite the good pay—and efficiency began to decline. Thus there were important reforms in this area especially. Although the Americans have now left, these reforms have remained.

The crews now spend several weeks on the job and then have a week's vacation. For this vacation, they are flown to recreational areas along the Mediterranean. Foreign workers are frequently flown to Europe. Back on the job, workers on the oil rigs put in long workdays—and long nights. Eight- to ten-hour shifts are the norm, and these shifts go on all around the clock since oil is pumped and drills are operated twenty-four hours a day. Top supervisors and administrative personnel usually work from shortly after dawn until shortly before lunchtime. To avoid the worst heat, they take the midday hours off, then return to work at three and continue working until dusk.

Under the blazing desert sun, outside the air-conditioned areas, dehydration is a constant threat. To avoid it, every day the workers each drink several gallons of distilled water heavily laced with salt. Despite all such discomforts and the more common dangers and hazards faced by oil-field workers everywhere, the ceaseless task of getting the black gold out of the ground and transported to an oil-hungry world goes on twenty-four hours a day, seven days a week, all year round.

WORLD PETRODOLLAR PROBLEMS

In at least one major way the Arab tribes and nations of the Middle East and North Africa have resembled those of the Indians of North America. They have been unable to establish and maintain long-term alliances, even in the face of a common enemy. In America, the great Indian chiefs Tecumseh and Pontiac each created alliances among tribes in the Midwest to fight the U.S. Army, but these alliances lasted only a brief period. Intertribal jealousies soon shattered them.

The Arabs have also united briefly from time to time. Perhaps the most notable Arab alliance took place during World War I under the British soldier and writer Thomas Edward Lawrence, better known as "Lawrence of Arabia." Colonel Lawrence welded together scattered Arab tribes and drove their European enemy, Turkey, out of the Middle East. But at the end of the war this alliance, like many before it, collapsed in a struggle for leadership.

The most recent attempt at an Arab alliance was begun not for military purposes but for economic ones. The alliance itself is a cartel, which is usually an association of businesses joined together to restrict the marketplace and fix prices. In this case, the cartel consists of thirteen nations, several of them non-Arabic.

The thirteen nations banded together in order to take control of petroleum production in their countries and set the world price of their exported oil. The cartel is called the Organization of Petroleum Exporting Countries (OPEC) and is made up of Algeria, Ecuador, Gabon, Indonesia, Iran, Iraq, Kuwait, Libya, Nigeria, Qatar, Saudi Arabia, the United Arab Emirates, and Venezuela.

In the beginning, OPEC seemed the most successful Arab-led alliance to date, but then it began to show signs of strain. Basically this strain was caused by disagreements between the "Hawk" OPEC nations, which wanted to continually raise the price of oil no matter what the market conditions were, and the "Dove" OPEC nations, which wanted to maintain relatively reasonable prices as well as low production levels to avoid a world oil glut. The disagreements over how to obtain the most so-called petrodollars over the longest period of time threatened to destroy OPEC.

The leading Dove OPEC nation has been Saudi Arabia, which has also tried to maintain good political relations with the U.S. government. One of the leading Hawk OPEC nations has been Libya, under the militant rule of Qaddafi. Since Saudi Arabia produces more oil and is the stronger of the two nations militarily, the Saudi position has prevailed. But Qaddafi and Libya do have some clout. For one thing, Libya produces a type of high-grade light oil that is much sought after in the West. This great demand for its oil helps make Libya a key OPEC member. Secondly, Libyan oil production has been almost completely nationalized under the Libyan National Oil Corporation (LINOCO). Foreign oil companies have had a relatively free hand in operating in other Arab countries. In Libya, they must get permission directly from LINOCO, and any agreement with LINOCO usually includes terms that give Libya 85 percent of all profits. Qaddafi has urged other Arab OPEC

OPEC ministers meet in Yugoslavia in June 1986
to decide on a standard price for their oil exports.

countries to take a similar stand in dealing with the West, and many of his fellow Arabs agree with Qaddafi's policies.

LIBYA'S PETRODOLLAR
PROBLEMS

Within ten years after oil was discovered in its desert region, Libya was producing about 7 percent of the oil used by the United States and the rest of the world. That figure remained steady until the early 1980s. Then it began to drop. When President Reagan took his firm stand against Qaddafi's terrorist activities, he also threatened to declare an embargo against Libyan oil, which he finally did on March 10, 1982. Since the United States received only a small amount—roughly 2 percent—of its foreign oil from Libya (it gets much more from Saudi Arabia), this did not create much of a hardship for Americans. But when the president suggested that Japan and western Europe go along with the embargo, he met with strong opposition. Japan and various European nations get a third of their oil supply from Libya, and it is extremely doubtful that they would go along with such an action except under the most extreme provocation.

Nevertheless, the U.S. embargo and the threat of a wider one was worrisome to Qaddafi and the Libyans. In addition, the Libyan dictator had other growing petrodollar problems.

When Qaddafi led the way in sharply raising OPEC oil prices following a brief cutoff in oil supplies to world markets in 1973, great riches began to flow into Libya. In 1970, Libyan oil sales amounted to roughly $1.3 billion. (This is the amount in American dollars. The Libyan currency is the dinar. There are about 3½ Libyan dinars to the American dollar.) In 1974, after the embargo and price increase, Libya's earnings for oil were some seven times greater than they had been in 1970. They remained at that high level throughout most of the 1970s. But then they began to slacken due to an oil glut brought about by generally poor economic conditions worldwide and conservation measures taken by oil consumers throughout the world.

Libya and Qaddafi had three basic petrodollar problems. The first two appeared almost immediately and in rapid succession; the third was longer in coming. First of all, there was the question of what to do with all the money being earned by the sale of Libyan oil. No sooner was this problem solved by massive expenditures on government programs to aid the populace than the second question arose—how to cut back on these programs when oil earnings began to falter. Billions of dollars spent on improvements on the home front had made Qaddafi popular. Would slashing these funds and halting improvements make Libyan citizens angry enough to revolt?

The third question was what to do when Libya ran out of oil. This question poses no immediate problem, but it is a real one for all OPEC nations and will one day have to be dealt with. When the internal combustion engine and the automobile replaced the horse and buggy, blacksmiths, buggy whip and harness makers, and buggy manufacturers went bankrupt by the thousands. Oil is a nonrenewable fuel, existing in limited supplies, and the day when it will run out is approaching. It is doubtful that there will be an end to automobile manufacturing. Instead, some alternative fuel will doubtless be discovered or developed. This time it will be the oil producers who could go bankrupt, and Qaddafi does not relish the idea of being the proprietor of a bankrupt nation. But a solution to that problem could be postponed. The first two problems were more immediate and had to be dealt with when they arose.

Libyan women march under a portrait of Qaddafi. They are training at the women's military academy in Tripoli.

First of all, Qaddafi used the increase in oil revenues to greatly strengthen Libya's military forces. Today, the Libyan army numbers about 55,000 men plus a so-called "people's militia" of several thousand civilians. All are equipped with the most modern weapons. The people's militia is composed of men past military age, women, and teenagers. The Libyan Air Force, with several thousand foreign-trained flyers, is equipped with modern French and Soviet jet aircraft—Mirages and MIGs. The Navy, though small, is equipped with several submarines and numerous small warships ranging from missile boats that resemble motor torpedo boats up to ships of the destroyer class.

Although the Libyan armed forces do not appear large in sheer numbers, they are indeed large in relation to the country's total population. In strengthening the army, however, Colonel Qaddafi may have created a monster that will one day devour him. To date, most of the signs of opposition to Qaddafi's dictatorship have come from within the military ranks, and some Western observers believe that one of the reasons Qaddafi sent his army into Chad was to keep the soldiers occupied outside the country and thus prevent them from toppling him in a coup as he and the rest of the Revolutionary Command Council had toppled King Idris. Following the bombing of Libya by the United States in 1986 there were also signs of unrest among Libyan military leaders.

CHANGES IN THE HOME-FRONT GOVERNMENT: A NEW CONSTITUTION

In 1977, Qaddafi replaced the old Revolutionary Command Council. He did so by presenting the country with a new constitution. Under this new constitution, Libya's government became, Qaddafi said, "a new form of direct democracy." The official name of the country was also changed. It became the Socialist People's Libyan Arab Jamahiriya. Jamahiriya means "state of the masses."

Since 1977, a General People's Congress of some one thousand popularly chosen delegates has met about twice a year. This Congress is theoretically the highest policy-making government body in the country. Its General Secretariat and General People's Committee execute national policy. The secretary of the General People's Committee is similar to a prime minister.

Under the new constitution, Colonel Qaddafi retained his position as "Leader of the Revolution." But neither he nor any of his Revolutionary Command Council took any formal job in the new government. Nevertheless, Colonel Qaddafi remained the dictator of Libya and the man in complete charge of all government activity. The People's Congress is no more than a rubber-stamp legislature when it comes to important matters of government policy.

IMPROVEMENTS IN
HOME-FRONT LIVING AND
WORKING CONDITIONS

Before the discovery of oil in Libya, the lives of the people were harsh. Rural life was especially severe, causing many farmers to flood into the towns and cities seeking work. Here they were forced to live in shanty-towns, called *barrakas*, because there was insufficient urban housing. Jobs, too, were scarce.

Many of those living in the *barrakas* were teenagers. Libya has a young population, with 50 percent of the people less than fifteen years old. Life expectancy is only about forty-seven years. Consequently, the *barrakas* became teenage ghettos, where many youths lived in mud huts or shanties built of scraps of sheet metal, wood, and tar paper. Through the glassless windows came the constant sound of transistor radios blaring forth music both day and night.

But soon the oil-rich Qaddafi government began to improve this picture. The *barrakas* disappeared, and in their place rose some 450,000 new single-family homes and multi-storied apartment buildings. On top of most of these buildings there were television antennas. The number of jobs increased. Not only was the housing construction business booming, but new factories appeared—factories that manufactured everything from chinaware to furniture. In the towns and cities, new shops appeared, built of glass, steel, and concrete, and across the desert and semidesert countryside, new, four-lane concrete highways were under construction. Other interior roads were greatly improved. As soon as this new transportation network was complete, brand-new imported automobiles began to appear on it. Throughout the country 400 million trees were planted.

Health services, utilities, and a variety of social services were provided where before there had been none. New public clinics and schools were opened, not just in the cities but even in small rural towns. Farmers who once barely scratched out a living on subsistence-level farming and by herding a few head of scrawny cattle now found agricultural conditions greatly improved. No government agency could provide rain in desert and semidesert areas, but government agencies could provide the machinery for digging deep new wells and expensive chemical fertilizer to make the desert area bloom.

City-dwellers, for whom unemployment had been a way of life, now found that there were jobs for everyone who wanted one. True, many of these were government-created jobs that did not actually fulfill a real need or result in the production of anything, but they paid good money.

In sum, within a few short years, Qaddafi's socialist government had virtually transformed Libya into nearly the ideal welfare state. But as in all such situations, there were some flaws, some cracks that began to appear in the picture window of the Libyan Socialist Republic, just as they had begun to appear in the windows of the new, jerry-built apartment buildings.

CRACKS IN
THE PICTURE WINDOW

For one thing, until relatively recently, Libya has had a virtually untrained work force as far as twentieth-century industrial standards are concerned. Because Libyans are largely untrained and unskilled, almost half of the nation's industrial workers have had to be imported from abroad. These workers have come largely from Egypt and central and southern Europe, especially Poland and Italy. Qaddafi's government has struggled to overcome this situation by offering free vocational and technical training to all Libyans who desire it, but to date, this effort has not been wholly successful. Despite compulsory and free education, Libya's illiteracy rate remains high—about 50 percent—and illiterate people rarely make good trainees. Illiteracy is decreasing, however. In the early 1970s it was 80 percent.

The government has also been faced with the problem of Libyans spending their money on luxury consumer goods manufactured abroad. The enormous number of imported transistor radios is a good example of this. But not just luxury goods are imported. Even many of the raw materials used in building new plants, homes, and apartment buildings have had to be purchased abroad. This causes a serious imbalance in the economy and prevents Libya from being as independent and self-sufficient as Qaddafi wants his country to be.

The lack of leisure-time activities is also a problem. Libyans with surplus money find little to spend it on by way of amusements such as sports contests, the theater, theme parks, vacation or recreational areas, and other spare-time activity outlets that are largely taken for granted in the Western world.

Libyans also have little incentive to save their money. Under Qaddafi's socialist regime, all savings accounts above 1,000 Libyan dinars—about $3,500— have been "nationalized," that is, taken over by the government. Nor are there incentives for investment such as in real estate. All homes and apartment buildings not actually lived in by their owners have also been nationalized, and private enterprise of all kinds has largely been eliminated.

In the summer of 1986, Qaddafi threatened to eliminate entirely the use of money in his country. What this would do to the Libyan economy if the plan were to actually be adopted is difficult to imagine. Certainly it would seriously complicate foreign trade.

Since the adoption of the new constitution, all factories, stores, and businesses have gradually been taken over by the state. They are now run by so-called People's Economic Committees. These are a form of collective management similar to that in the Soviet Union and other Iron Curtain countries. Theoretically, this is a highly democratic way of doing business, but as has been proven time and again in all socialist countries, it breeds confusion and inefficiency. When everybody is running a business, nobody is running it. And when there are no incentives such as promotions, increased pay, and increased authority offered for operating a business well and at a profit, managerial indifference becomes a way of life.

Nevertheless, up until the early 1980s, Qaddafi's socialist government remained relatively popular because oil revenues were spread so generously among the Libyan people. Then the world oil glut forced Libya to face a fifty percent cut in its oil production and income. This came at a serious time for Qaddafi; he and his government had recently started their most important program to date—a five-year development plan that was to turn Libya into a showplace nation. The budget for this new plan was more than $60 billion, and it was based on predictions of a steadily rising oil income. Obviously, the budget for this program had to be severely trimmed.

Included in the proposed budget was money for additional oil exploration. Petroleum engineers and geologists estimate that Libya has already used up as much as one-third of its known oil reserves. If this is true, then sooner than he has anticipated, Qaddafi may have to face the question of what to do when the oil runs out. And if no more oil is found in Libya and the people are faced with the prospect of returning to their old standard of living, a new chapter may begin in Libya's long and troubled history—a chapter in which Muammar Qaddafi may become just a footnote.

FOUR

A BRIEF HISTORY
OF LIBYA

All of northern Africa except Egypt was called Libya by the ancient Greeks. In the seventh century B.C., Greek colonists occupied the region in today's Libya that is still called Cyrenaica. At that time Cyrenaica had much more rainfall than it has now. Because of this, agriculture flourished, and the capital city of Cyrene became a Greek center of trade. Cyrene also became a cultural center. The philosopher Aristippus founded the Cyrenaic school of philosophy and education, which taught that "pleasure tempered by intelligent moderation" was the ideal lifestyle.

Cyrene grew to a city of some 100,000 people. Archaeologists have since found many of its ancient marble baths, temples, and burial grounds long covered over by the desert sands. In the fourth century B.C., Cyrenaica fell to the Egyptians and somewhat later was taken over by the Romans.

Rome used Libya largely for growing grain—mostly wheat. It used this grain to feed its numerous military legions as well as the populations of Rome itself and much of Italy. Archaeologists have also found the ruins of several ancient Roman cities in Libya, mainly along the Mediterranean coast.

One of the most important of these cities uncovered by modern archaeologists was Leptis Magna. It was once ruled by the Emperor Septimius Severus and was regarded by the Romans as one of the most beautiful of all their colonial cities. Leptis Magna and the two nearby cities of Sabrata and Oea were often spoken of as Tripoli, or "The Three Cities." This is how the area of Libya that is today called Tripolitania as well as the nation's capital city got their names.

In the fifth century A.D., barbaric hordes from the Baltic region began to plunder Europe. These barbarians were called "Vandals," a name that still survives today and applies to those who recklessly destroy private property. In about A.D. 428, the Vandals crossed the Strait of Gibraltar and moved into Africa. According to legend they were encouraged to come to Africa by a discontented Roman governor of one of the African provinces. If the story is true, it was a fatal mistake, for within ten years the Vandals had conquered all of northern Africa's Roman provinces.

But the Vandals failed to conquer Egypt or any other African country. For almost two centuries, the Egyptians waged war against the invaders and finally drove them out of Africa. The Arabs then overran all of the former Roman colonies and took control of the area that is now Libya. The former Roman colonies, however, had become increasingly undesirable possessions. Gradually the climate had become drier, and crops could no longer be grown there, except in areas bordering the Mediterranean. It is believed that Libya's climate reached its present state sometime during the late Middle Ages.

THE BARBARY STATES

During the eleventh, twelfth, and thirteenth centuries, various European powers sent a series of military expeditions to Africa to try to recapture the Holy Land,

Christ's birthplace, from the Muslims—mainly the Turks. These Christian military expeditions, which ended in failure, were called the Crusades. When they were over, many of the Crusaders settled on the Mediterranean islands of Rhodes and Malta and in the Libyan city of Tripoli. Tripoli had been taken over by the Catholic King Ferdinand of Spain in 1510, and Ferdinand encouraged the Crusaders known as the Knights of St. John to occupy the city. They did so until 1551, when they were driven out by the Turks.

Under the Turks, all of northern Africa from Egypt to the Atlantic Ocean was called the Barbary Coast. Four of the countries that occupied the Mediterranean coast—today's Morocco, Algeria, Tunisia, and Libya— were called the Barbary States. The term *Barbary* comes from *Berber*, the name of a group of Hamitic tribes that once occupied much of northern Africa. Today in Libya the Berbers have largely been absorbed into the Arab population, although there are still many of them in North Africa. Half of Morocco's population, for example, is Berber-speaking.

THE BARBARY PIRATES

Gradually, the Barbary states became a pirate stronghold. North African piracy on a small scale dated back to ancient times, but beginning in the sixteenth century, the Turks and the Moors of Morocco turned it into big business. In fact, at one time in the first half of the seventeenth century, there were said to be as many as 25,000 prisoners captured by the pirates and held for ransom in Tripoli, Algiers, and Tunis. In addition to prisoners, the captains, or *raises*, of the pirate ships took so much plunder that they were able to form corporations to conduct their businesses for them.

At first, the Barbary pirates used galleys to carry on their brigandage. These were relatively small ships with

*Pirates from Algiers and Tunis terrorized
the Barbary coast for many years.*

slaves who manned the oars in long galleys just below
the main decks. The heads of the various pirate corporations, who were called *beys* or *aghas*, paid for these
ships, hired the *raises* to captain them, supplied the galley slaves, and did whatever additional outfitting was
necessary. In return, the *beys* or *aghas* received 10
percent of the value of whatever prizes were captured.
The *raises* and the crews hired by the *raises* divided up
the rest of the spoils on a prearranged basis. Galley
slaves, of course, got nothing.

In the seventeenth century, a Dutch sailing master
by the name of Simon Danser deserted his country's
merchant fleet and joined the Barbary pirates. Danser
brought with him a knowledge of how to build and operate sailing ships. Ships under sail were not only much

faster and more maneuverable than those manned by galley slaves, but they also could be larger and thus hold much more booty. Consequently, the pirate corporations soon began replacing the smaller galleys with huge sailing ships. The latter were far more costly, but the return on investment in them was greatly increased.

Among the private citizens captured by the pirates it was usually only the rich who were freed after a ransom was paid for them. Some of the poorer captives were freed if they denied their faith in Christianity and accepted the Islamic faith. Most of the poor, however, were simply condemned to slavery. Some even became galley slaves in the pirate ships before the galleys were replaced by sailing vessels.

During the eighteenth century, the Barbary pirates became so powerful that they began to demand tribute from foreign countries that wanted to sail their ships through the Mediterranean unharmed. One of the countries from which such tribute was demanded was a brand-new nation—the United States of America.

Having just won one war, the American Revolution, partially caused by England's demand for tribute in the form of stamp taxes on tea and other English exports to America, the fledgling United States was not about to pay tribute to a motley horde of pirates along the far-away Barbary coast. In fact, it would be another dispute over freedom of the seas that would soon lead the United States into a second war for independence against England—the War of 1812. "Millions for defense, but not one cent for tribute," was an American battlecry of this whole era.

TO THE SHORES OF TRIPOLI

Actually, between the end of the American Revolution and the turn of the nineteenth century, the United

States had already paid the Barbary pirates some $2 million in ransom for American seamen captured while sailing in the Mediterranean. This money was paid reluctantly, mainly to save American lives. But when the *bey* of Tripoli informed the United States that its ships would now have to pay tribute simply to sail freely through the Mediterranean, President Thomas Jefferson surprised everybody by going to war over the matter. The newly elected U.S. president was a peace-loving man, but he firmly believed that this was too high a price to pay for peace. His sentiments were to be somewhat echoed by the newly elected President Reagan in Reagan's response to Qaddafi's lawless actions almost two centuries later.

Thomas Jefferson became president of the United States in 1801 and almost immediately set about building up the American Navy for war against the Barbary pirates or anybody else who threatened freedom of the seas. This was not Jefferson's first experience with the Barbary pirates. Before becoming president, he had been the American ambassador to France. He had taken one of his two daughters, Martha, to live with him in Paris, leaving his other daughter, Maria, with her aunt in the United States. Later, he sent for Maria to join him and Martha in France. Then he worried for weeks while she was making the long voyage over; her ship, which was scheduled to dock in southern France at Marseille on the Mediterranean, might be boarded at any time by pirates who might capture Maria and hold her for ransom. Jefferson had been told that the pirates often received secret information about the children of diplomats who were scheduled to sail the Atlantic, and several of these children had been taken. Maria arrived safely in France, but Jefferson never forgot the worry the pirates had caused him.

For a time after he became president, Jefferson tried to deal with the *bey* of Tripoli through diplomatic

Commodore Edward Preble (left)
and Lieutenant Stephen Decatur

channels, but when these efforts failed and the *bey's* pirates continued to prey on American shipping in the Mediterranean, Jefferson dispatched a U.S. Navy task force to the shores of Tripoli. This was early in 1804. The task force consisted of the man-of-war *Constitution*; several frigates, including the *Enterprise* and the *Philadelphia*; and several light gunboats. In command of the task force was Commodore Edward Preble.

Preble was born in Portland, Maine, in 1761. He had run away to sea at sixteen and had served with the Massachusetts state navy during the Revolutionary War. A fearless sailor and warrior, Commodore Preble also had in his task force an equally fearless and daring young naval officer, Lieutenant Stephen Decatur. Decatur was in command of the *Enterprise*. Later, he was to be remembered for his famous toast: "Our country—in her relations with foreign nations, may she always be right; but our country, right or wrong." The *bey* of Tripoli was to remember Decatur for other reasons.

Decatur had been too young to fight in the American Revolution. He was born in 1779 in a log cabin in Sinepuxent, Maryland. However, he was a veteran of the sea, having made his first voyage at the age of eight when he sailed on a merchant ship captained by his father. He had joined the U.S. Navy in 1798 and quickly rose to the rank of lieutenant, his official rank on the *Enterprise*, although he actually captained the ship.

When the commodore's task force arrived in the harbor of Tripoli, Preble immediately ordered his ships to open fire on the *bey's* fortress, located on a point of land overlooking the harbor. Soon much of the fortress was reduced to rubble, and Preble ordered his ships to withdraw. Unfortunately, on leaving the harbor, the frigate *Philadelphia* went aground on a reef. Shortly afterward, the *bey's* forces imprisoned the crew of the marooned *Philadelphia* and floated the frigate off the reef in order to prepare to use it themselves.

That night, on February 16, 1804, Commodore Preble called on Stephen Decatur aboard the *Enterprise* to see if he thought he and his men could recapture or at least destroy the *Philadelphia*. Decatur agreed to try. Immediately, he and his men slipped secretly back into the harbor, boarded the *Philadelphia*, overwhelmed the sleepy crew, and set the ship afire. The *Philadelphia* burned to the water line. Then Decatur and his boarding party, not one of whom had been killed and only one of whom had been slightly wounded in the raid, returned to their own ship and escaped out of the harbor. Despite fire from the more than one hundred guns in the Turks' now-aroused shore batteries, Decatur's raiders remained virtually unscathed.

The burning of the Philadelphia *in 1804*

Upon hearing of Decatur's exploit in Tripoli harbor, the famous English admiral Horatio Nelson called it, "The most bold and daring act of the age." Later, Decatur was awarded a sword by the U.S. Congress for his bravery and promoted to the rank of captain at the age of twenty-five. He was to go on to even greater glory during the War of 1812.

THE MARINES HAVE LANDED

While the shores of Tripoli were being assaulted by U.S. Navy gunships, an attack against the land side of the city was also being planned by the U.S. Marines.

The Marines had been created by the Continental Congress in 1775 to fight in the Revolutionary War. They were then allowed to go out of existence after the Revolution but in 1798 were reactivated by Congress as a separate military service within the U.S. Navy establishment. Now they were to return to action.

The land attack against the Tripoli pirate stronghold was organized by William Eaton, the American consul at Tunis, capital of Tunisia. Eaton had long opposed paying tribute to the Barbary brigands, many of whom used Tunis as a base from which to sally forth and prey on foreign shipping in the Mediterranean. Eaton had even opposed paying the pirates ransom for captured American sailors. Although Commodore Preble's task force might successfully bombard Tripoli, Eaton knew that American ground forces would have to capture the city to put the Tripoli pirates permanently out of business. And if Tripoli fell, then perhaps Tunis and Algiers, the other two pirate strongholds, could also be captured.

Eaton conferred with his superiors in the United States and was given permission to go ahead with the proposed operation if Commodore Preble agreed. The American naval commander in the Mediterranean gave his consent and even supplied Eaton with some of his Marines for the operation. These included Lieutenant Presley O'Bannon to command the mini-army and a squad of enlisted "Leathernecks." (The nickname came from the heavy leather stock, or collar, that the Marines wore to protect their necks from saber and cutlass blows.)

The Navy also supplied one naval midshipman to the expedition and forty Greeks who had worked aboard U.S. ships when they were in Greek ports. On his own, Lieutenant O'Bannon managed to round up about one hundred foreign soldiers of fortune plus a squadron of Arabs who wanted to drive the *bey* of Tripoli out of the country. The Arabs brought with them their own camels, and O'Bannon bought enough additional camels to transport about half of the rest of his force across the desert. Those without camels walked.

Eaton planned the route that the Marine-led attack force was to follow. Lieutenant O'Bannon thought the attack should be launched from Tunis, but for some reason Eaton insisted that Egypt be the jumping-off point. (Perhaps he feared that if it began in Tunis the *bey* of Tunis might get wind of the operation and alert the *bey* of Tripoli.) In any event, O'Bannon and his men were ordered to march from Alexandria, Egypt, to Derna, Libya, some 500 miles (800 km) away. They were then to march on to Tripoli, another 500 miles further westward.

When the march began, on March 6, 1805, Eaton rode along on his camel side by side with Lieutenant O'Bannon, at the head of the column. Having spent several years in the Middle East, Eaton was accustomed to riding camelback. Unfortunately, he was the only American in the party who was. The Marines and the lone midshipman were accustomed to the swaying decks of ships, but these four-legged "ships of the desert" were another matter.

The camels were tireless, but the motion-sick Americans aboard them were not. Frequently the Marines simply got off and walked, leading the camels. The beasts were also difficult to care for. They were the most mean-tempered animals the Americans, many of whom were former farmboys, had ever seen. Finally, all of the camels were put under the care of the Arabs, who were accustomed to them. This caused severe grumbling among the Arabs, who objected to doing double duty, and several near-mutinies resulted. With a combination of tact and firmness, Eaton and O'Bannon smoothed things over and persuaded the Arabs to continue the march.

Most of the early part of the journey was through the burning sands of the Sahara. By day the sun blazed in a cobalt-blue sky, and the men wilted in the heat. By night severe cold gripped the desert, and the shivering men had to huddle together beneath the brightly shining stars to ward off the chill. Several times food and water ran low, but the Arabs led the party to desert oases, where supplies were replenished.

It took a month to reach Derna. The expedition arrived at the outskirts of the city on April 27 and almost immediately began the attack. At the first sound of gunfire, three American warships that had been standing offshore waiting for this signal also began to bombard the city and its central fort. Lieutenant O'Bannon and his Marines led the charge on the fort itself, which fell almost immediately. The surprise nature of the attack undoubtedly had something to do with the fort's quick surrender. Had the defenders known how small the attacking force was, they certainly would have held out longer.

Only a short time later, Eaton and O'Bannon were

ceremoniously raising the American flag over the fortress. This would mark the first time that the relatively new flag of the recently born United States would be flown over an Old World city.

Eaton was eager to push on to Tripoli, but now various diplomatic moves began to be made. When he received word that Derna had fallen, the *bey* of Tripoli sued the United States for peace. In return, he promised to mend his piratical ways. Pressure for peace was also brought to bear by several European nations. In the end, no further U.S. military efforts in the area were authorized, and the American forces were evacuated from Derna.

Eaton was so incensed over the decision not to press on and try to end piracy once and for all in the Mediterranean area that he resigned from the consular service. And the Barbary pirates continued for a time to prey on passing ships. It was not until some years later, in fact, that piracy in the area finally and completely died out. Stephen Decatur had a hand also in the Barbary pirates' final demise when at the end of the War of 1812 he returned to the shores of Tripoli with a squadron of U.S. Navy ships and bombarded the last of the pirate strongholds into submission.

But the capture of Derna taught both the Barbary states and all of the Old World nations respect for the New World's newest nation and flag. In addition, the U.S. Marines later commemorated the occasion by including in their official hymn the line, "From the halls of Montezuma to the shores of Tripoli." The halls of Montezuma referred to the Marines' exploits during the later Mexican War.

No U.S. Marines were involved in the U.S. attack on Tripoli and Benghazi in 1986, but the air strike was a reminder that the United States was now not only a prideful nation but also a powerful one. President Reagan made it clear that American military forces would

not back away from the challenge presented by Qaddafi's "Line of Death" any more than the youthful United
States had backed away from the challenge of the Barbary pirates.

LIBYA UNDER THE ITALIANS

Colonial empires controlled by European nations
reached their peak during the late 1800s. Before World
War I began in 1914, two of the Barbary states, Algeria
and Tunisia, had come under the control of the French.
Morocco was controlled by the French and the Spanish. Libya continued to be ruled by the Ottoman Turks
until 1911, when the Italians, following in the footsteps
of their Roman forebears, drove out the Turks and
made Libya an Italian colony.

At about this time, there began within Libya a strong
movement for independence. Before leaving the country, the Turks had granted the Libyans "full and entire
autonomy." This was largely an empty gesture, however, since the Italians were about to take over the whole
country. Soon the Libyans found themselves ruled by
still another foreign power.

During World War I, Italy went to war against Turkey
once again, this time on the European mainland.
Because it was badly in need of troops for the conflict,
Italy withdrew its forces from most of Libya, continuing
to occupy only the major coastal cities. Again, the
Libyans began to hope for independence. But when
World War I ended in 1918, those hopes were
dashed.

Libyans wanted their country to become a republic
or a monarchy, but Italy wanted to recolonize the area
and keep it under strict Italian control. Libya was
allowed to become a limited monarchy, and the regions
of Tripolitania and Cyrenaica were permitted to have
their own parliaments. These parliaments, however,

served under Italian governors. The region of Fazzan retained its semi-independence.

In the early 1920s, changes began to take place in the governments of several European countries. In Italy, Fascism came into power. The Italian Fascists under dictator Benito Mussolini ("*Il Duce*") were nearly as ruthless in their treatment of minorities as Adolf Hitler and his Nazis later were in Germany.

Count Giuseppe Volpi was replaced by a Fascist general, Rodolfo Graziani, who set out to establish a military dictatorship in Libya. Graziani subdued Tripolitania by 1923 and Fazzan by 1929. Cyrenaica continued to resist somewhat longer, but it also fell, in 1932. Graziani anticipated Hitler in the use of concentration camps. All Libyan political dissidents, including most of the population of Cyrenaica, were herded into these grim compounds, where many died.

Officially back in the fold as an Italian colony, Libya was actually an Italian military base even before the start of World War II in September 1939. But in the several years preceding the war, Mussolini sent some 30,000 Italian colonists into Libya in an attempt to build it up as a model Fascist colonial outpost. To make the area more attractive to the colonists, the Italian government spent vast sums of money to develop it.

This money was used for new irrigation projects, new buildings, new roads, and new and improved harbors. The ports of Tripoli and Benghazi were rebuilt. A huge naval base was established at Tobruk, which had one of the best natural harbors in North Africa. Bardia, another excellent port city, was developed into a modern metropolis. A fully paved highway was built along the entire length of the coast, and other roads were extended to the oases in the south. Several new airports were also constructed. All of these last improvements were to play an important role in World War II.

The Italian colonists were not to remain in Libya

long enough to enjoy the delights of *Il Duce's* model colony. As soon as the war began, most of them were evacuated and returned to the Italian mainland.

LIBYA DURING
WORLD WAR II

Libya was a major theater of war during World War II. It was here that such names as Germany's "Desert Fox," General Erwin Rommel, and British generals Bernard Montgomery and Archibald Wavell and the armies they commanded—Germany's *Afrika Korps* and Britain's Army of the Nile and Eighth Army (the legendary "Desert Rats")—were to be written large in military history. And it was to be in Libya at such places as Bardia, Tobruk, and Benghazi that some of the most important battles of World War II would be fought.

Libya was important in the war because of its strategic location. Germany and Italy had formed an alliance before the war called the Rome-Berlin Axis. When both Italian and German military forces occupied Libya at the start of the war, the two Axis powers controlled the southern Mediterranean. Great Britain still held Gibraltar at the mouth of the Mediterranean as well as the island of Malta. But Germany had overrun Greece and captured the island of Crete, so the Axis also controlled the Mediterranean from the north. With most of the Mediterranean thus in Axis hands, supplies to support British forces in the Middle East had to be sent all the way around the Cape of Good Hope at the southern tip of Africa.

The main goals of the Axis were to control the Suez Canal in Egypt and the oil-rich lands of the Middle East. Oil was vitally needed, of course, to keep the Axis war machine running, just as it was vital to the Western Allies. Since oil had not yet been discovered in Libya, that country was seen as merely a potential pathway to the countries that did have oil. To reach the Suez Canal and the oil fields, the best starting point for the Axis was the Libyan-Egyptian border.

In September 1940, the Italians, under General Graziani, invaded Egypt. Graziani predicted to Mussolini that the victory would be an easy one. But at Sidi Barrani, the Italians encountered Britain's General Wavell, a veteran desert fighter who had learned his skills serving with T. E. Lawrence in World War I. Wavell commanded the Army of the Nile, a mixed force of British, Australian, and New Zealand (Anzac) troops numbering some 40,000 men. Before the year was out, Wavell and his mixed forces had not only driven the Italians out of Egypt and back into Libya, but they had also taken more than 35,000 prisoners. It was largely from this debacle that the Italians gained their World War II reputation as, in Wavell's words, "a somewhat second-class foe."

Wavell pressed on into Libya after the retreating Italians and attacked them at Bardia. The Anzacs led this assault, and the results were the same. Bardia quickly fell, and the bag of Italian prisoners was even greater than at Sidi Barrani, some 45,000 dispirited Italians.

The British under Wavell wasted no time. They pushed on to Tobruk, the main Italian naval base in Libya. Though delayed somewhat by sandstorms, they reached their destination, and within a few weeks, Tobruk fell. Then in quick succession Derna and Benghazi were taken. At Derna, the site of America's first Old World conquest, the British captured not only many more prisoners but also, and more importantly, a valuable supply of water.

ENTER THE DESERT FOX

But then there was a sudden shift in fortunes. Just when it seemed that the British might overrun the whole

*General Erwin Rommel during an inspection trip
in the North African desert in June 1941*

of Libya and drive the Italians out of North Africa, the Germans came to the aid of their shaky ally. A well-equipped and well-trained armored corps arrived at Tripoli, the most important city in Libya. The commander of this crack *Afrika Korps* was General Erwin Rommel, soon to be nicknamed the "Desert Fox."

In two months, the British desert army had conquered most of North Africa, from Sidi Barrani to Benghazi, and captured more than 100,000 prisoners. More important, the Suez Canal was no longer threatened. But this would change with the entry of Rommel onto the desert stage.

Rommel was a master of mechanized, or *panzer*, warfare. He soon proved himself to be a master of desert warfare as well. Aided by a large force of *Luftwaffe* fighter and bomber aircraft, Rommel smashed the British into sudden retreat. Starting in late March 1941, Rommel's mechanized divisions retook Derna and Bardia and were at the gates of Tobruk within ten days.

Wavell was forced to withdraw most of his forces from Libya and return to Egypt. At Tobruk, he left a strong force of Anzacs, with instructions to hold out for two months—if possible. With unbelievable courage and against overwhelming odds, the "Rats of Tobruk" held out for eight.

Rommel's *blitzkrieg*, or lightning attack, and Wavell's hasty withdrawal from Libya cost the British several thousand prisoners, including three generals. But worst of all, the Suez Canal was again threatened. The British, however, would return, this time with their new ally, the United States.

THE YANKS ARE COMING

Rommel had to delay any new Axis attempt to capture Suez until he could build up his supply and troop reserves. This delay proved to be a long one. In the spring of 1941, Germany invaded Russia, and all German supplies and manpower were diverted to that front for many months.

The United States entered the war when the Japanese attacked the American naval base at Pearl Harbor, Hawaii, on December 7, 1941. At first it was assumed that the United States would concentrate its major war efforts against Japan, in the Pacific theater of war. Instead, President Franklin D. Roosevelt and his military chiefs of staff decided to make the European theater their first priority. Once this was decided upon,

North Africa soon became the primary target of the Western Allies, the United States and Great Britain. They agreed that it was essential to wrest North Africa from the hands of the Axis so that the Suez Canal would be freed for Allied use. North Africa could then also be used as a base of attack upon the European continent via Italy and southern France.

The invasion of North Africa—called Operation Torch—was planned for the fall of 1942. Landings were planned in Morocco and Algeria, west of Libya. If Torch was successful, Rommel's forces would be trapped between Torch invaders advancing eastward and British forces in Egypt advancing westward. The final showdown might well occur in Libya.

Meanwhile, however, Rommel and his *panzer* divisions threatened to destroy all of these fine Allied plans. Rommel had been resupplied and reinforced, and early in 1942 he began another invasion of Egypt from Libya.

First, Rommel's *Afrika Korps* recaptured Libya's besieged bastion of Tobruk. This was just one of several times that this vital Mediterranean seaport was to change hands during the course of the war. Then Rommel entered Egypt and launched an attack against General Auchinlech. At this point, there seemed to be nothing between Rommel and the Suez Canal. But the British Eighth Army made a heroic stand at El Alamein, just a few miles west of Alexandria. A siege developed that lasted for weeks. In the end, El Alamein proved to be a high point in the war for the British, and its defenders became heroes.

ENTER MONTY AND
THE DESERT RATS

In August 1942, just as the Torch invaders were sailing for Africa, General Montgomery took command of the

Eighth Army. On October 23, he ended the siege of El Alamein by launching an all-out counterattack. Using several hundred American Sherman tanks that had recently been delivered to Egypt's Port Said, "Monty" and his "Desert Rats," as they were affectionately called by the British, soon began to drive Rommel's *Afrika Korps* in defeat toward Libya.

The goal of Monty and his Desert Rats was Tobruk, the hub around which any successful North African campaign would have to turn. In November 1942 the Eighth Army successfully recaptured Tobruk, thus forging the first link in what was hoped would be a chain of victories leading to final triumph in North Africa.

The Torch operation began on November 8, 1942, under General Dwight D. ("Ike") Eisenhower. Ike made Britain's Rock of Gibraltar his headquarters for the invasion. Landings were made near Casablanca in Morocco, and Oran and Algiers in Algeria. The Americans who landed at Casablanca had sailed directly from the United States. Those who landed at Oran and Algiers had sailed from England.

The invasion of North Africa took the Germans and Italians completely by surprise, but they immediately began to build up their forces in Libya and Tunisia, where they suspected the next major battle would be fought. Rommel asked for and received 150,000 additional troops plus the war matériel to supply them. The Allied buildup also continued. By early in 1943, the Americans had some 200,000 additional men ashore as well as hundreds of thousands of tons of supplies.

Meanwhile, Rommel had continued his retreat westward through Libya before the determined advance of the British Eighth Army. Soon Rommel's *Afrika Korps* and his massive reinforcements joined at a series of defenses along the Libyan-Tunisian border called the Mareth Line. Rommel now had Montgomery on one

Left: *Newspapers on November 8, 1942, announce the landing of the American forces in North Africa. This was the beginning of the all-important Operation Torch.* Below: *Field Marshal Viscount (earlier General) Montgomery ("Monty") with Lord Alexander, defense minister of England, and General Dwight D. Eisenhower in 1952.*

side of him and three American divisions on the other side.

But the crafty Desert Fox was not finished fighting. Far from it, in fact. He now turned suddenly on the Americans and soundly defeated them at a place called Kasserine Pass. This was the first heavy fighting the American troops had engaged in, and the green GI's panicked in the face of Rommel's seasoned veterans. About 200 Americans were killed in this February battle, but more than 2,000 were wounded and some 2,500 were taken prisoner.

THE END OF THE AXIS
IN NORTH AFRICA

The Americans learned fast, however. Within a matter of days of their defeat at Kasserine Pass in Tunisia, the Americans rallied. Rommel was driven back through the pass. In March, Montgomery's Eighth Army overwhelmed the Mareth Line, and Rommel's forces were trapped and began to surrender. Rommel himself was relieved of his command and flown back to Germany, where he would live to fight another day during the Allied invasion of Normandy.

The remaining Axis forces in North Africa now had their backs to the sea and were hammered relentlessly by the Allies. All of Libya was soon held by the British and the Americans. Within a matter of months, the whole African continent had been swept clean of the Axis powers. Soon the Mediterranean had also been cleared for Allied shipping, and the way lay open for the invasion of Italy and the rest of southern Europe. The end of World War II was still many months away, but the tide of victory was now turning in favor of the Allies, and it was a tide that would eventually overwhelm the Axis powers.

FIVE

LIBYA'S ROLE IN
POSTWAR AFRICA

When World War II ended in 1945, the ideas of freedom
and independence began to sweep across the African
continent. Britain's Harold Macmillan, who was later to
become prime minister, perhaps expressed it best
when he said, "The wind of change is blowing through
Africa."

At the start of World War II, only three African coun-
tries were independent. These were Egypt, Liberia, and
South Africa. In the decades since then, forty-eight
former European colonies became free countries.
Libya, a former colony of Italy, was the first to do so, on
December 24, 1951. Under the mandate of the United
Nations, Libya declared itself a constitutional and
hereditary monarchy.

Achieving any real form of democracy in government, however, was not so easy. The difficulty in Libya,
as in most modern newborn nations, stemmed from the
people's apparent inability to govern themselves. Most
Libyans were without education. Many could not read
or write. Their lives had been governed by foreign powers, and they were not used to acting on their own ini-

tiative. This created a political vacuum in which it was relatively easy for a strong individual to become a dictator.

Great Britain showed the most wisdom and care in turning over its former colonies to native populations. British administrators continued on the job until local leaders and bureaucrats could learn how to handle the machinery of government. Other former colonial powers—France and Belgium, for example—either forced the colonies to fight for their independence, as in Algeria, or simply moved out virtually overnight and let the colonies fend for themselves, as in the Belgian Congo (today's Zaire).

Libya presented a somewhat different situation. After the Axis powers were driven out of the country during the war, Britain and France took joint control of it. Some Libyans and their leaders formed a strong attachment to the British as their liberators and benefactors. This was especially true of King Idris and his followers, who came into power when Libya became an independent monarchy. King Idris's British leanings were accepted for several years by most top Libyans but resented by others. In addition, the Idris regime had become quite corrupt as well as almost completely out of touch with the young Libyan nationalists who wanted complete independence for their country. Among the latter were Muammar Qaddafi and his military colleagues who deposed King Idris eighteen years after independence. Once Qaddafi came to power, he preached a fierce nationalism and did his best to end Libya's dependence not only on Britain but also on all other foreign powers.

Libya could not, of course, be truly politically independent until it was economically independent. Thus, the discovery of oil within Libya's borders in the late 1950s was of vital importance. Before the discovery of oil, not much was possible politically. After its discovery, all things were.

THE OTHER SIDE
OF THE QADDAFI COIN

When Qaddafi first became known to the Western world he was seen as the idealistic young nationalist leader trying to gain independence for his country. His people also felt this way about him. Unfortunately, it is not the way the West as well as most Libyans and Africans feel about him today. To begin with, the Libyans wanted a strong leader to direct their fortunes. Secondly, Qaddafi has always been a true nationalist and wise enough to realize that his people's destiny depended on revolutionary improvements in their education, health, and general standard of living. A Muslim religious zealot, Qaddafi has also crusaded for his people's welfare.

In addition, Qaddafi does not confine his dreams of betterment to the territory within his own borders. His dreams extend to the entire Arab world.

One of the pan-Arab groups Qaddafi is most dedicated to is the Organization of African Unity (OAU), to which most African nations belong. He has played host to the OAU and was expected to become its head in 1982. He did not become chairman of the OAU, however, mainly because many Africans felt he had been too meddlesome in the internal affairs of other Saharan countries. This rejection by other African leaders has increased Qaddafi's frustration and may be the cause for some of his continued erratic actions.

But despite his rejection, under Qaddafi's direction, Libya also contributes substantial sums of money to the Arab-controlled Development Bank for Africa, the Arab Fund for Technical Assistance to Africa, and the Islamic

Development Bank. Involvement in the last organization stems from Qaddafi's religious convictions. While doing business with non-Muslim nations, the Libyan dictator has tried, with a complete lack of success, to convert the presidents of the nations of Chad, Togo, Zaire, Sierra Leone, and Rwanda to Islam.

These leaders, although somewhat irritated by Qaddafi's persistent attempts to convert them, have nonetheless expressed their admiration for him and his interest in African affairs. They have also praised his support, financial as well as verbal, of worldwide liberation movements—in Ireland and the Philippines, for example. What most Western observers regard as Qaddafi's and Libya's support of terrorism is regarded by many African leaders as a commitment to national liberation.

At one time, Qaddafi even went so far as to provide a refuge in Libya for Idi Amin, the murderous deposed dictator of Uganda. This, too, was seen as a grand gesture by some black Africans. But when Amin was impolitic enough to refer to Libyan troops as "a bunch of women" because they would not help him regain control of Uganda, Qaddafi sent him packing. Amin then found refuge in Saudi Arabia.

A DIFFERENT VIEW OF LIBYA'S INTERVENTION IN CHAD

Several African leaders have also seen a positive side to Libya's intervention in the civil war in Chad in 1980. This war, they point out, had been going on for fifteen years before Qaddafi appeared on the scene. Qaddafi only intervened, they insist, at the request of the beleaguered President Woddei.

But in June of 1982, rebel forces in Chad led by Hissen Habre captured the capital and forced President

Woddei to flee the country. Qaddafi immediately sent in Libyan troops to oppose the Habre forces.

Qaddafi's actions caused both the United States and France to raise strong diplomatic objections, and France responded by sending in several thousand troops to support Habre and oppose the Libyans. After much negotiation Libya and France agreed to a simultaneous withdrawal of troops from Chad in the fall of 1984.

Many Africans regarded Qaddafi's act of sending Libyan troops to Chad as both a generous and effective one. It was only through Libya's intervention that the civil war there was at least temporarily ended and order restored. While they were in Chad, the Libyan troops suffered severe casualties. The fact that Qaddafi has no lasting interest in Chad, his apologists insist, was indicated by the fact that he promptly withdrew his troops when President Woddei requested him to do so in 1981. And further, they point out, Qaddafi had consistently approved and supported the formation of the Transitional Government of National Unity (GUNT), which was supposed to keep the peace in Chad. Qaddafi insisted that if GUNT, in conjunction with the OAU, was able to fulfill this peacekeeping role, he would remain out of Chad in the future. His supporters believed him.

QADDAFI AND THE BOMB

Generally speaking, however, world leaders outside of Africa are dubious about the strongman of Libya—his past, present, and future role in world affairs. One of the reasons for this is Qaddafi's persistent efforts to acquire nuclear weapons. If Qaddafi is a peaceful man, they have wondered, what does he want with the atomic bomb? As one United Nations member observed, "The same question, of course, might be asked of the NATO nations and the Soviet Union, but then such a question is not regarded as polite in superpower society."

In any event, for many years there have been rumors that Qaddafi would give a million dollars in gold—no questions asked—to anyone who would provide him with an atomic weapon. This money, according to rumor, is already deposited in a Swiss bank, where it awaits someone to claim it.

Whether or not these rumors are true, it is a fact that Qaddafi has been actively seeking the bomb since 1974. In that year, Libya began its nuclear program by signing an agreement with Argentina on the "peaceful uses" of atomic energy. Under this agreement, the two countries would work together prospecting for uranium in Libya. In return, Argentina would help Libya with development of its nuclear energy program. Just what sort of help Argentina has since provided is not known. Experts estimate, however, that Argentina itself will be capable of producing a nuclear bomb by the late 1980s.

Libya has received the greatest amount of help in its nuclear energy program from the Soviet Union. Since the mid-1970s, several small reactors have been built in Libya under Soviet supervision, and teams to run them have been trained by the Russians. Another reactor, which is still under construction along the Mediterranean coast, will be capable of producing enough fissionable waste material (plutonium) for the manufacture of up to twenty bombs a year. Qaddafi insists that the reactors are intended only to produce energy for Libyan utilities. Not everyone believes him.

In the late 1970s, Qaddafi called upon France and India for additional aid in developing Libya's nuclear energy program. Despite the promise of an increased supply of Libyan oil at bargain prices, neither country would agree to help Libya if it intended to build nuclear power plants for anything but peaceful uses. Tentative arrangements were made for Libyan students to study the management of nuclear power plants in Indian schools, but the deal fell through when Qaddafi made it clear that he also expected help in building nuclear weapons. India was suspicious of Libya's close ties with Pakistan, a country that for many years has feuded with India.

LIBYAN STUDENTS
IN AMERICAN SCHOOLS

Qaddafi has also used the United States in his quest for the bomb. Until recently there were at least two hundred Libyan nuclear engineering students at colleges and universities within the United States. Since several of the schools at which the Libyans were enrolled have nuclear research and development (R&D) programs funded by the U.S. government, this situation caused considerable alarm.

U.S. intelligence agencies tried to keep Libyans out of these R&D programs, but some school administrators intervened, complaining that the federal government was interfering with academic freedom. The Libyan students claimed that they were being trained to operate their country's nuclear energy programs, but there are far more nuclear engineers being trained in the United States, Europe, and the Soviet Union than could possibly be needed in any peaceful nuclear program. Today Libyan students are no longer permitted to study nuclear engineering or aviation in the United States.

There are also many scientists and nuclear engineering students in the United States who come from Arab nations other than Libya. Qaddafi's "recruiting squads" have carried on an active campaign to enlist these nuclear scientists in the Libyan weapons development program. However, few of these recruiting efforts have been successful, since those who were being recruited frequently reported the fact to their governments, who in turn reported this information to the Federal Bureau of Investigation. In fact, it was this attempted Libyan infiltration of the American scientific community that had alerted both the FBI and the CIA to Libya's potential subversive activity some time before rumors began to surface that Qaddafi's hit squad was about to extend its terrorist activities to the United States.

QADDAFI RECRUITS
FORMER CIA AGENTS

One recruiting effort in which Qaddafi was extremely successful involved the hiring of several former members of the CIA to train terrorists in Libya. These ex-CIA agents, in turn, recruited more than forty members of the U.S. Army's Special Forces—Green Berets who were in training at Fort Bragg, North Carolina—and transported them to Libya as a training cadre for the terrorist school.

The apparent leader of this terrorist operation was Francis E. Terpil, a member of the CIA for more than six years—and perhaps, some people think, a member still. After he reportedly left the CIA, Terpil became a shadowy figure who worked for several foreign intelligence services—including Britain's Scotland Yard military intelligence branch—and supplied arms, ammunition, and sophisticated explosives to several revolutionary governments. As an international firearms dealer, Terpil had among his clients Libya's Qaddafi.

Born and raised in Brooklyn, New York, Terpil discovered at an early age that there was an enormous profit to be made in buying and selling illegal weapons. When he was fifteen, young Terpil bought a machine

Francis E. Terpil, former CIA agent turned adviser to Muammar Qaddafi, speaks on the CBS program "60 Minutes."

gun from a policeman for a few dollars, and sold it for ten times that to the son of his high school science teacher. Terpil was soon arrested for this transaction, but he escaped with only a mild reprimand.

In 1958, when Terpil was eighteen, he joined the army, mainly because that was where the guns were. He served in the army for seven years, when he was recruited by the CIA. Sent to the CIA's so-called dirty tricks school at Langley, Virginia, he learned all the modern methods of sabotage, guerrilla fighting, and clandestine warfare. He was also taught special methods of assassination—rigging electric toasters with explosives, turning ballpoint pens into handguns, making lethal weapons out of safety pins by dipping them in cobra venom, and much more.

In 1970, at the age of thirty-one, Terpil was stationed in New Delhi, India. There, he decided to increase his income from his clandestine CIA duties by dealing in the money black market. Rupees bought with American dollars in India could be traded for afghanis in Afghanistan at a highly favorable rate of exchange. Back in India, the afghanis could again be redeemed for rupees and then changed into dollars at an enormous profit. Terpil soon found he was on the way to becoming a rich black market money merchant.

But in 1971, when war broke out between India and Pakistan, Terpil found himself stranded in Afghanistan. Since he had no official reason for being away from his post in India, he had to confess his black market activities to his CIA superiors. He was immediately shipped back to Langley and apparently resigned from the CIA in 1972.

A short while later, Terpil turned his dirty-tricks training and experience to profitable use as a freelance intelligence agent and international arms merchant. Over the next several years he was employed by Egypt, Iraq, Iran, Uganda, and Syria. He became a close friend of Uganda's dictator, Idi Amin, was acquainted with the South American assassin, Carlos the Jackal, and finally went to work for Qaddafi and Libya.

Terpil and Qaddafi met when Terpil and another ex-member of the CIA, Kevin Mulcahy, became partners in an organization called Intercontinental Technology. Through this company, Terpil supplied Qaddafi with explosives and a wide variety of terrorist equipment, material that Qaddafi could not have obtained on his own. Terpil worked with Qaddafi from 1976 to 1980. It was during this time that the Libyan terrorist training school was organized.

During the latter part of this period, Terpil's agents began recruiting American soldiers from among the Green Berets at Fort Bragg. The implication was that the entire operation had CIA approval. With this under-standing, the Green Berets' Luke Thompson took five of his men plus 800 pounds (360 kg) of plastic explo-sives to Libya. There Thompson found Terpil in charge of training Libyan military personnel for foreign terrorist assignments. In time, the original handful of Green Ber-ets grew to a total of forty-three.

For a variety of reasons, however, Luke Thompson became suspicious of the Libyan operation. He returned to the United States, where he reported to the Army's counterintelligence people. He was then told that the activity in which he had been engaged was not a CIA-approved operation. Soon afterward, the rest of the Green Berets returned to the United States, but they as well as the CIA have since maintained a discreet silence concerning their activities in Libya.

In 1980, Terpil returned to the United States, sup-posedly on a visit but apparently on clandestine busi-ness. That same year, he and another ex-CIA agent, Edwin P. Wilson, were indicted for violating federal laws by shipping explosives to Libya. Also indicted but on lesser charges was a third American, Douglas M. Schlachter.

Terpil was free on bail when he and another col-league, George G. Korkala, were arrested by New York undercover police for offering to sell them terrorist arms and ammunition. In September, Terpil, again free on bail, and Korkala fled the United States for the Mid-dle East. They were later tried in absentia and sen-tenced to fifty years in prison.

Terpil and Korkala were last seen in Beirut, Leba-non. From there, in September 1981, Terpil offered to make a deal with the U.S. Congress. He would return from exile and tell his entire story, including the naming of everyone he had been involved with, if federal charges against him were reduced.

Shortly after Terpil made this offer, he and Korkala

were reportedly visited by several Syrian secret service agents. Immediately after this, Terpil and Korkala disappeared and have not been seen since. American agents have speculated that Terpil and Korkala might have been assassinated to keep them from talking. Or they may have been spirited away to Libya where, under Qaddafi's protective wing, they await a more favorable international climate before they surface again.

Terpil's colleague in crime, Edwin P. Wilson, did not escape American justice. He, too, fled the United States shortly after he was indicted but was later lured into the Dominican Republic, where he was seized by American law enforcement agents and returned home for prosecution. Today he is serving a fifty-two-year prison sentence in the Marion, Illinois, federal penitentiary.

Born in Idaho in 1928, Wilson grew up in a poor family. While still in his teens he joined the merchant marine and then the Army. In 1955 he joined the CIA. In the CIA he became a secret, or covert, agent running a clandestine company that shipped weapons and electronic gear to pro-American countries throughout the world.

But in 1971 the CIA stopped sponsoring Wilson's company, and shortly afterward Wilson reportedly quit the agency. He did not end his arms dealings, however. In fact, he soon began selling his services to the highest bidder, in this case Libya's Colonel Qaddafi. Working with Terpil, Wilson sold Qaddafi American-made guns,

Ex-CIA agent Edwin Wilson leaves a federal courthouse after being sentenced to fifteen years in jail and fined $200,000 for smuggling weapons into Libya.

airplane parts, bomb detonators, and an additional 21 tons of the terrorist's favorite plastic explosive, C-4.

Wilson also helped Qaddafi set up the training camps to teach the Libyans how to use these supplies and even made futile attempts to procure for Qaddafi an atomic bomb. But Wilson's activities did not go unnoticed. An assistant U.S. attorney for the District of Columbia, Lawrence Barcella, began tracking Wilson through his American contacts and after four long years of effort managed to run him to ground in 1982.

Wilson was lured out of Libya, where he was living in stylish comfort in a villa in Tripoli, by a promise of a deal. He was told he would be able to obtain a suspended sentence on the illegal international trafficking in arms charge. His capture and subsequent sentence to prison soon followed his return to the United States. At the time of his conviction Wilson was a multimillionaire.

One of the major questions that has arisen from this case was whether or not Terpil and Wilson actually ever left the CIA. Intelligence experts have been quick to point out that one of the most popular devices for infiltrating an enemy operation is to have one's own agent apparently defect to the enemy. Then, once inside the enemy operation, the agent can report back to his or her own intelligence people just what the enemy is up to. Terpil and Wilson, in other words, may never have resigned or been fired from the CIA. It may all have been a pretense to enable them to infiltrate the military operations of other countries—especially Qaddafi's terrorist training school—so they could report back to the CIA. Otherwise, it has also been asked, how could the U.S. Army have allowed key members of its Green Berets unit—many of whom have traditionally been members of the CIA—to leave Fort Bragg, journey to Libya, and then return with little or no comment about their activities there?

These and many other questions may, of course, never be answered.

WAS REAGAN CRYING WOLF?

One of the questions that many Americans found themselves asking with increasing frequency early in 1982 was whether there really had been a Libyan crisis, with Qaddafi sending out a hit team of political assassins. Were President Reagan and his administration guilty of crying wolf? And if so, to what purpose?

Certainly, the original assassination rumors had been real enough. And their confirmation by the White House had caused a great stir in the press and on television. But for weeks and months after the first scare, there was no official comment. News on the subject suddenly became nonexistent. It was as if the assassination story were a nightmare that official Washington preferred to forget.

Then, in mid-January 1982, the FBI announced that it had opened an inquiry into a possible link between the attempted assassination of Pope John Paul II on May 13, 1981, and the Libyan hit teams that had reportedly targeted President Reagan. The FBI inquiry grew out of a statement made by a Detroit man, Lowell Newton, who thought he recognized a picture he had seen of one of the alleged Reagan hit men. Newton said he was "reasonably sure" that the man pictured was the same man he had seen with a gun in his hand running away from the fallen pontiff moments after he had been shot. Newton even said he had taken a photograph of the fleeing suspect.

Newton and his wife had been on a vacation trip to Rome in the spring of 1981. Along with thousands of others, they were in St. Peter's Square when the pope was shot by a Turkish terrorist named Mehmet Ali Agca. Agca was captured moments after the assassination attempt, and at first it was assumed he had acted alone. However, Newton said that he and his wife had seen a second man carrying a handgun running toward a Vatican Square exit immediately after the incident. Newton had taken a picture, but it showed the man only from behind, with his face in half-profile. It did not show the gun.

Newton later gave his evidence to a judicial committee in Rome that was investigating a possible conspiracy in the attempt on the pope's life. Several European news magazines claimed there had been a conspiracy, and that Libyan terrorists were involved. Back home, Newton said no more on the matter until *Time* magazine in its December 21 issue ran drawings of several men who were suspected of being members of the Libyan hit team that may have entered the United States in November. At that time, Newton thought he recognized one of the drawings as the fleeing gunman he had seen and photographed in Rome. Newton said, however, that he couldn't be 100 percent sure "from just the one crude drawing."

Nevertheless, the FBI thought enough of his story to launch a full-scale inquiry. Newton's eyewitness account and photograph plus the drawing of the suspect in *Time* suggested not only a Libyan conspiracy in the attack on the pope but also a link between that attack and the Libyan hit team reported to be stalking President Reagan.

POSSIBLE ADDITIONAL LIBYAN LINK TO ITALIAN TERRORISTS

One of the most notorious of all world terrorist organizations has been Italy's so-called Red Brigades. In 1978, the Red Brigades kidnapped and killed the former Italian premier, Aldo Moro, and they have been involved in numerous other vicious terrorist activities since. Late in December 1981, the Red Brigades captured a high-ranking U.S. Army officer, Brigadier General James L. Dozier. Out of this kidnapping grew accusations by a Rome judge that Libya was connected with the Red Brigades.

General Dozier, fifty, was the chief of logistics and administration for the North Atlantic Treaty Organization (NATO). His headquarters were in northern Italy, in the city of Verona. He and his wife lived in a nearby apartment; Dozier was kidnapped from there. The Red Brigades announced that they were responsible for the abduction and that Dozier would be held for a "people's trial." After that, there was no word about him for many weeks. Investigators scoured Italy for the missing general but to no avail.

In mid-January 1982, the Italian investigating judge, Ferdinando Imposimato, accused Libya and the Soviet Union of providing arms and other support to the Red Brigades. Judge Imposimato based his accusations on statements made by jailed Italian terrorists cooperating with police. He documented his charges against the Red Brigades with sworn testimony from some forty-eight terrorists who had taken part in earlier kidnappings and killings. These Red Brigades members also said they were sure the gang had already killed General Dozier.

RESCUE BY THE "LEATHERHEADS"

But on January 28, after forty-two days of being held prisoner, General Dozier was rescued by Italian police commandos who stormed an apartment in Padua and overpowered the general's Red Brigades captors. Dozier was unharmed, but he narrowly escaped being killed at the very moment of his rescue. When the raiders smashed down the door of the "people's prison," one of the kidnappers had a pistol pointed at the general's head. Before the kidnapper could fire, however, the pistol was knocked out of his hand with a karate kick by one of the rescue commandos. Later it was disclosed by Italian officials that the terrorist who was holding the pistol to Dozier's head when police burst into the room had been in Libya during 1981, undergoing paramilitary training.

General Dozier was the first kidnap victim of the Red Brigades to escape with his life. His rescue was accomplished by a highly skilled, ten-man police squad specially trained in antiterrorist tactics. Officially, the squad's name is the Central Operative Nucleus of Security (NOCS), but the members are popularly called "Leatherheads" because of their riot helmets, which resemble the leather headgear worn by ancient Roman gladiators. They also wear masks, and their identities are kept strictly secret. The man who kicked in the door to the Padua apartment, however, is generally believed to be Italy's champion weight lifter.

General Dozier was unstinting in his praise of the Leatherheads. "I'd be proud to have them on my team," he said. After a two-week period of debriefing by Army Intelligence, the general also said he was eager to return to his NATO duties. Although no details were given, it was disclosed that General Dozier had supplied valuable information on the tactics and operations of the terrorists.

Regarding his own reaction to the ordeal, General Dozier first quoted a poster he had seen when he had served in Vietnam during the war: " 'Those who have never been required to make sacrifices for freedom don't know the true value of freedom.' The events of the past six weeks or so were just my one small sacrifice on behalf of freedom. These sacrifices continue."

While General Dozier was being held captive, another U.S. Army officer serving in Europe, Lieutenant Colonel Charles R. Ray, had made the supreme sacrifice. Ray, an assistant military attaché in the U.S. embassy in Paris, was shot and killed by a lone assassin on January 18, 1982, while on his way to work. The killing of Ray, forty-three, followed by five weeks a similar but unsuccessful attempt on the life of another embassy diplomat, Christian Chapman (see Chapter 1, page 18).

Immediately after the attempt to kill Chapman, U.S. Secretary of State Alexander M. Haig, Jr., said that Washington had indications that Libyan assassination squads were behind it. Haig made no comment after Ray was killed except to express sympathy for Ray's family.

President Reagan also expressed sympathy and said that the United States was making every effort to end such senseless slaying by infiltrating terrorist organizations to learn their plans ahead of time in order to thwart them. After the Dozier kidnapping, Reagan also expressed a considerable amount of wrath regarding the cowardice of all kidnappers and killers. In this, he said, he knew he was speaking for all Americans.

AMERICA'S HANDS
NOT CLEAN

The only trouble with such a statement was the fact that the United States did not have clean hands itself when it came to assassinations and assassination attempts on foreign heads of state.

Following the passage of the Freedom of Information Act by the U.S. Congress in 1966, investigative reporters learned that the CIA had secretly enlisted organized crime to kill Cuban dictator Fidel Castro during President John F. Kennedy's administration. Kennedy had wanted Castro overthrown because of the dictator's ties with the Soviet Union. Following an abortive, U.S.-backed invasion of Cuba at the Bay of Pigs, the CIA, probably without Kennedy's knowledge, issued a contract on Castro's life. The crime syndicate, or Mafia, accepted this contract through one of its bosses, Sam Giancana. The Mafia was also eager to get rid of Castro so it could reestablish its gambling operations in Cuba, which Castro had shut down when he took control of the country.

None of the Mafia's assassination plans were successful, perhaps because Castro learned about them and referred to them in several radio broadcasts. After President Kennedy's assassination on November 22, 1963, there were widespread rumors that Castro had had Kennedy killed in retaliation for the threats on his own life, but no evidence for this was ever found.

After he succeeded Kennedy as president, Lyndon B. Johnson learned of the plans to kill Castro as well as other CIA assassination efforts. Johnson's comment was that the CIA was "running a damned Murder, Inc., in the Caribbean." One of the incidents Johnson was referring to was the assassination on May 30, 1961, of Rafael Trujillo, dictator of the Dominican Republic. There were strong indications that the CIA had supplied the guns to Dominican dissidents for this murder.

The CIA was also linked to the overthrow during the Vietnam War and perhaps the subsequent death of Ngo Dinh Diem, president of South Vietnam. The U.S. government definitely wanted Diem deposed despite the fact that South Vietnam was America's ally in this conflict. Diem was deposed in November 1963, largely as a result of efforts by the CIA; the CIA may also have played a role in Diem's subsequent assassination.

President Reagan did not refer to these or any other unsavory examples of American involvement in international terrorism, but Libya's Qaddafi did not hesitate to do so. In December 1981 and January 1982, the Sudan News Agency reported that two unsuccessful attempts had been made on strongman Qaddafi's life. In one assassination attempt Qaddafi was slightly wounded in the jaw but otherwise unharmed. Both would-be assassins were dissident army officers, and both were killed by Qaddafi's guards. Afterward, the Libyan dictator accused the CIA of having infiltrated the Libyan Army and instigating the plot. Qaddafi pointed out that this was not the first time the CIA had tried to assassinate a revolutionary foreign leader, citing the attempts on Castro's life as a prime example.

The White House as well as U.S. intelligence agencies refused to comment on Qaddafi's accusations. But at that time Reagan did try hard to get legislation passed that would have put curbs on the U.S. Freedom of Information Act. This would have prevented future disclosures of any U.S.-sponsored assassination attempts.

QADDAFI ACCUSES THE UNITED STATES OF PROVOKING WAR

Qaddafi, however, continued to talk. Early in March 1982, in a speech before a forum of labor and political groups in Libya, he accused the Reagan administration of provoking him into a war "that cannot be won unless the United States drops an atomic bomb on Libya."

Vowing that he would die "spitting in America's face," Qaddafi added that if the U.S. Sixth Fleet again entered the Gulf of Sidra, "it will mean war because it entered our territory. War in its full meaning will flare up between us involving the air force, the navy, missiles— everything. We have been patient with the United States and its daily lies and accusations," the Libyan leader concluded, "but it is not the policeman of the world or our guardian." In mid-March, Reagan announced he was cutting off all oil imports from Libya and would not sell any high-technology American equipment to Libya. Qaddafi admitted to the press that the cut-off would hurt him but said he would not give in to American attempts to isolate him in world affairs.

After all of these threats Qaddafi's reactions were surprisingly mild when the United States did reenter the Gulf of Sidra and actually bomb his country in the spring of 1986. Perhaps one of the reasons for his silence was that the specific purpose of the U.S. air raid was actually to kill Qaddafi. U.S. officials denied that this was the case, but there were many observers who thought otherwise. If this was the case, then the raid had failed in its key purpose, and there was reason for Qaddafi to speculate that another attempt on his life might be made by an American hit squad. Consequently, he might have decided just to maintain a low profile for a few months.

SIX

QADDAFI'S AND
LIBYA'S FUTURE

In the mid-1980s, Libya's immediate future seemed to be almost wholly dependent upon Qaddafi's future. And Qaddafi's future seemed largely dependent upon how long Libya's oil would hold out and how much of a demand for it there would continue to be—not just in the West but throughout the world.

It was clear that there was a certain amount of unrest among the Libyan civilian population as cutbacks were made in social betterment programs following a prolonged drop in oil revenues. This, of course, might eventually lead to Qaddafi's downfall. Early in 1982, for example, there were persistent reports from travelers coming out of Benghazi that troops had been called out to put down civil disturbances in that eastern Libyan city. One report said there had been a number of civilians killed and at least five hundred arrests, including those of several hundred students. In countries outside the United States it has frequently been among students that revolutions have begun.

Following the American bombing of Tripoli and Benghazi in 1986, civilian unrest was again reported. Although Qaddafi tried to channel this reaction into anti-

Libyans demonstrating and chanting anti-American slogans in the streets of Tripoli after the U.S. raid which destroyed parts of the city

American demonstrations, many of the demonstrators also expressed their dissatisfaction with the Qaddafi regime.

An attempt at expansionism might also be made by Qaddafi to take the heat off his domestic problems. This is a traditional move made by dictators in trouble at home, and one that Qaddafi may already have used once in entering into Chad's difficulties. In 1982, a number of Libyan officials were reported to have arrived in Accra, the capital of Ghana. On New Year's Eve there had been an attempted coup in Ghana. The coup had failed, but Qaddafi had evidently seized upon it as another golden opportunity to "volunteer" Libyan aid in propping up a threatened neighboring regime. Whether or not the Ghanian government would accept such aid from the Libyan strongman was, of course, another question.

IS OPEC A "PAPER TIGER"?

In the end, Qaddafi's and Libya's fortunes will probably rise or fall along with those of the other Arab nations in OPEC. And OPEC's future depends on whether or not its members can maintain their unity as a cartel in the face of the world oil glut. There are those experts who claim that OPEC is merely a paper tiger that will eventually be destroyed by a civil war among its members over a diminishing petroleum market. Other experts, to be sure, stoutly disagree. In the summer of 1986 the OPEC nations did manage to agree to cut their oil production by 4 million barrels a day. Immediately oil prices soared throughout the Western world. But there was a serious question as to whether or not this OPEC accord would last. Several money-hungry OPEC nations, including Libya, threatened to produce as much oil as they wanted to and sell it at whatever the market price would bring.

Is there indeed a diminishing market for OPEC oil? There certainly seems to be in the United States. During the 1980s the United States imports of foreign oil dropped by almost one-half. Imports from Libya fell from 7 percent to less than 2 percent. However, imports still made up almost 40 percent of total American oil consumption. During that same year, the United States consumed an average of 5.7 million barrels per day of imported oil and 8.6 million barrels per day of domestic oil.

There were several reasons for this decline, not all of which were permanent. Energy demands were sharply reduced temporarily by a severe economic recession. This recession became even more severe in 1982. But when the recession ended in the mid-1980s oil consumption increased only by a modest amount. Energy conservation as a result of consumer resistance to higher oil prices, the development of more fuel-efficient automobiles, solar heating, and other alternate energy sources will undoubtedly carry over into the future and even increase. Government decontrol of oil prices also helped stabilize domestic production and will undoubtedly increase it in the future. Decontrol of natural gas prices may be an additional aid in this area.

One oil company study estimates that by 1990, the United States will be importing only 31.6 percent of the petroleum it uses. This study also predicts that in the year 2000, oil consumption in the United States will still be below the level of oil use in 1973. That was the year of the first OPEC oil embargo. The reduction will be accounted for almost entirely by a cutback in oil use, the study adds.

A similar situation in worldwide oil use has also been forecast. But there is great disagreement on this subject, even within the petroleum industry. Those who say that the apparent worldwide oil glut is merely a temporary oversupply insist that the situation could give way at any time to major oil supply disruptions.

Some experts say that the only hope for the future of an energy-hungry world is an energy-diversified economy. This means an all-out effort to develop a wide variety of energy sources other than oil. But this will take time. Meanwhile, the prospect is that the Organization of Petroleum Exporting Countries will continue for many years to be a major source of the United States' and the world's oil supply. Thus, it would appear that Libya and its strongman, Muammar Qaddafi, will be forces—for good or for evil—to reckon with for the forseeable future.

AFTERMATH OF THE
U.S. RAID ON LIBYA

Meanwhile, one further question was being asked: Did the bombing of Libya by the United States end Qaddafi's export of terrorism? The answer seemed to be a qualified yes. At least there were no massive reprisals on the part of Libya, as many, including members of the Reagan administration, had feared. There simply was no short-term wave of retaliatory terrorist activity.

According to the U.S. State Department, during several months preceding the raid, terrorists were responsible for killing six Americans and wounding sixty-six. In the several months following the raid two Americans were killed by terrorists and two were wounded. What might happen in the long run remains to be seen.

AFTER QADDAFI WHAT?

One of the things that might well happen in the future, observers agree, is the overthrow of the Qaddafi regime. It is quite possible, in fact, that Qaddafi may be assassinated not by foreign assassins but by his own people. In any event, as Middle East expert Lisa Anderson has observed, "Qaddafi seems unlikely to die in bed."

And who would be responsible for such a coup? Probably the military. Although there seems to be very little likelihood of a "widespread popular uprising against the regime," according to Anderson, "the only plausible source for a change in government is the military, and the makers of any successful coup may or may not find kindred spirits among the exiled opposition."

Today there are some 50,000 Libyans living outside the country. Among these Libyan expatriates are many former business and political associates of King Idris whom Qaddafi deposed. Many of these exiles in Saudi Arabia, the United States, and Great Britain still have close ties with friends in Libya. Although these exiled members of the former elite could scarcely hope for a return of the monarchy, it is quite conceivable that they might support a military coup that would enable them to return to Libya under a new regime.

There are also a number of conservative nationalists within Libya who feel that the Qaddafi regime has become far too radical in both its domestic and foreign policies. These conservative nationalists favored the overthrow of the corrupt Idris regime and the removal of Western influences from Libya—specifically the American and British air bases there. They were not, however, social revolutionaries who favored the redistribution of wealth from oil revenues among all of the people of the country, as Qaddafi had originally attempted to do. Nor have they favored Qaddafi's radical revolutionary approach in foreign affairs, which included the diplomatic break with Egypt.

These conservative nationalists still want to see increased support for business rather than the elimination of capitalism, as Qaddafi has also attempted. They also want a strong, independent Libya but one that gets along with its Arab neighbors rather than alienates them and isolates Libya. The conservative nationalists, at no small risk, founded an organization called the Democratic Front or Movement in 1979 and began publishing a magazine called the *Voice of Libya*. Since then this group has merged with several other groups of defectors from the Qaddafi regime, a coalition that offers a serious threat to the Libyan leader.

But none of this opposition is capable of overthrowing Qaddafi without the military. If the military should defect and carry out a successful coup, it will undoubtedly be strongly supported by the overseas Libyans as well as the conservative nationalists and their allies at home. Whether or not such a partnership could succeed in establishing a stable Libyan government after Qaddafi is, of course, questionable. What could easily happen, as has happened in similar situations involving a military-civilian coalition elsewhere, is a constant round of coups and countercoups until a new dictator steps in and temporarily establishes order. The prospects, therefore, for domestic and political tranquility in Libya's future look none too bright.

FOR
FURTHER
READING

Anderson, Lisa. "Assessing Libya's Qaddafi." *Current History*, May 1985.

_____. "Qadhdhafi and His Opposition." *The Middle East Journal*, spring 1986.

_____. *The State and Social Transformation in Tunisia and Libya, 1830–1980.* Princeton, N.J.: Princeton University Press, 1986.

"Economic Survey." *New York Times*, February 5, 1978.

Facts on File, 1981–82.

Field, Michael, ed. *Middle East Annual Review.* Essex, England: Saffron Walden, 1981, 1985. Distributed in the United States and Canada by Rand McNally.

Khadduri, Majed. *Modern Libya.* Baltimore: Johns Hopkins University Press, 1973.

Lawson, Don. *Morocco, Algeria, Tunisia, and Libya.* New York: Franklin Watts, 1971.

"Libya's Hit Teams." *Time*, December 21, 1981.

Maas, Peter. *Manhunt.* New York: Random House, 1986.

McKown, Robin. *The Colonial Conquest of Africa.* New York: Franklin Watts, 1971.

Micallef, Joseph V.R. "A Nuclear Bomb for Libya?" *Bulletin of the Atomic Scientists*, August–September, 1981.

Paxton, John, ed. *The Statesman's Yearbook, 1981–82, 1985–86.* New York: St. Martin's Press, 1981, 1986.

Sheehan, Edward. "Colonel Qadhafi: Libya's Mystical Revolutionary." *New York Times Magazine*, February 6, 1972.

"Special Report: Qaddafi's Libya." *Christian Science Monitor*, December 11, 1981.

United States Department of State. *Background Notes: Libya.* Washington, April 1977.

"Why Reagan Moved Against Libya's Qadhafi." *U.S. News and World Report*, December 21, 1981.

World Topics Yearbook. Lake Bluff, Ill.: United Educators, 1982, 1986.

INDEX